Low-Carb & Gluten-Free
VEGETARIAN

SIMPLE, DELICIOUS RECIPES FOR A LOW-CARB AND GLUTEN-FREE LIFESTYLE

Low-Carb & Gluten-Free
VEGETARIAN

SIMPLE, DELICIOUS RECIPES FOR A LOW-CARB AND GLUTEN-FREE LIFESTYLE

Celia Brooks

Photography by Clare Winfield
Nutritional analysis by Fiona Hunter and Anita Bean

METRO BOOKS
New York

contents

introduction

"Have you heard about this great new diet? No third helpings." Stanley Kubrick

It was Stanley Kubrick's wife Christiane who first got me started on this book, nearly ten years ago when I wrote the original version. Back then, I was cooking for her, her family, and friends nearly every week, so when several of them decided to try a low-carb diet, it was time for me to get my low-carb thinking cap on. This is the result of many months' experimenting, learning, feasting, and losing weight!

This is not a diet book, it's a cookbook. That said, it's a cookbook mainly for those who have embraced the low-carb lifestyle that is set to dominate the Western world in the 21st century, especially as refined carbs and sugars become more and more demonized by health experts. The low-carb diet has undergone criticism, but there's no doubt it works for those who stick to it. Surely obesity is more dangerous? There's an awful lot of conflicting information out there, but one point nutritionists will agree on: controlling carbs reduces appetite, and if you eat less, you will lose weight.

To be true to this project, I went on a low-carb diet myself. I had been a normal, healthy weight for several years and didn't have much weight to lose, but I have had plump phases in my life and I know how fabulous it feels to get thin. What I really wanted was to "live the low-carb life" to get a clearer picture of what the diet is really like. I was surprised! Almost immediately, I noticed that my appetite shrank. I was snacking less and eating smaller meals. I really did feel that my mind was more focused and I had sustained energy levels. I could sit at my desk for hours without even thinking about what I would wander into the kitchen to nibble on next. Unlike other diets, there was not a sense of deprivation or longing. After two weeks, my clothes felt loose and I had lost about 3 pounds. This proved to me that the diet works.

I think it's the stereotype of the "fat chef" that often prompts people to ask me, "How do you stay so slim?" My reply is always the same. "Plenty of exercise!" Whatever diet you're on, that's the key. I advise anyone embarking on a low-carb diet to read the books that are out there and decide what's right for them. Pair that up with increased physical exercise, and you have nothing to lose but excess weight.

Developing these recipes was a whole new experience for me. I established a finite set of ingredients that were low-carb and vegetarian. Within that realm, I applied the same passion and relish as I always do, aiming to create the most sumptuous dishes I could muster. I hope this cookbook will contribute some ideas to your repertoire, vegetarian or not, low-carb or not, and that the recipes are as fun to cook as they are to eat. It's good food. Enjoy!

Celia Brooks, 2013

how it works

There are two factors that make the low-carb diet unique: The first is insulin control. When you eat carbohydrates, the body quickly converts them into the basic sugars of which they are composed. The presence of these sugars in the bloodstream gives you a surge of energy, but also triggers the pancreas to produce insulin. Insulin's job is to enter the bloodstream and remove the sugars for storage as fat. This happens fast, and once the insulin has stored the sugars, your appetite returns. It follows that if you eat fewer carbs, your body doesn't have the sugars there to burn for fuel, so it resorts to the fat stores, and off drops the excess weight.

The second factor is how protein affects appetite. Carbs burn up quickly while protein takes longer to digest. So a high-protein meal, with plenty of tofu or eggs, for example, will leave you feeling fuller for longer. You are then less likely to snack between meals and end up eating less overall. If you do feel like a snack, you'll get more mileage out of a high-protein one.

Protein is the obvious stumbling block for a vegetarian on a low-carb diet. It is assumed that the diet is too limiting without meat or fish. While it would be impossible to follow a no-carb diet as a vegetarian (and this would be discouraged from a health point of view), there are actually plenty of high-protein, low-carb options available, especially eggs and tofu, and they both dominate the recipes in this book. Because of the high vegetable content of many of the recipes, I would argue that going low-carb vegetarian could be one of the healthiest diets around. After all, vegetables are the elixir of life.

PROTEIN

Protein is your best friend on a low-carb diet. Many vegetarian protein sources, except nuts and cheese, are also low in fat, which increases your chances of successful weight loss. Not only that, all natural vegetarian protein sources are rich in other nutrients that can improve your general health. Beans and legumes are protein-rich, but they are also carb-rich. Having set myself the challenge of creating recipes with just 10 g carbs or less per serving, I found it best to leave these out of the recipes, but, along with whole grains, they should form part of a balanced diet and can be consumed in moderation if you are not being too strict with your carb count.

EGGS

Eggs are often referred to as "the perfect protein." As with all other animal protein sources, they contain all twenty amino acids that form a complete protein, all wrapped up in a neat little shell. Eggs contain many beneficial minerals and vitamins, including vitamin E—a natural antioxidant that helps prevent disease. While the belief has long been held that the cholesterol in eggs is unhealthy, doctors and health organisations no longer advise restricting egg consumption. Studies have found no relationship between dietary cholesterol or egg consumption and heart disease risk.

I can't stress enough the importance of buying organic eggs. Not only do organic chickens have a happier life in their freerange surroundings, but their diet is totally vegetarian and free of chemicals, antibiotics, and hormones. On a low-carb vegetarian diet, your egg intake will be high. Since what goes into the chicken goes into the egg, which then goes into you, organic is the only way to go. Yes, they are a little bit more expensive, but only by a fraction, and well worth the small extra investment.

SOY

The mighty soybean is Nature's gift to vegetarians. It is one of the only plant sources of complete protein (as with animal protein, it too contains all twenty amino acids). Soybean products are low in fat and carbs, high in protein and disease-preventing antioxidants, and also high in plant estrogens, which have many benefits, including reducing the risk of breast cancer. In fact, the USFDA recommends that everyone incorporate at least 25 g soy protein into their daily diet, to help reduce cholesterol levels. While most natural foods lose their good qualities and nutrients in processing, the opposite is true of soy. A cake of processed tofu has more concentrated nutrients than the raw bean, and fewer carbs weight for weight. As with eggs, organic soy is best. Be aware that nonorganic soy is often genetically modified.

NUTS

Nuts and seeds are little powerhouses of nutrition. They are high in protein and also boast a high vitamin E, fiber, and mineral content. Brazil nuts contain high levels of selenium, which is particularly beneficial for vegetarians because it's one of the only plant sources of this essential mineral. Nuts score high in the fat department, but it's good, unsaturated fat. Walnuts are one of the few plant sources of omega-3 fats, the cholesterol-lowering fats found in oily fish.

DAIRY

There are many low-fat dairy products available, but they almost always contain a higher carb count. A scant half cup (3½ fluid ounces) of low-fat yogurt contains 7.4 g carbs, while the same quantity of thick and creamy Greek-style yogurt contains just 4.8 g. Reduced-fat crème fraîche generally contains zero or very low carbs, so I've used that in some of the recipes.

As a general rule of thumb, the higher the fat content of the dairy item, the lower the carbs—butter and most cheeses contain none. All dairy foods are products that have been processed, so always check the nutritional information on the packaging, in case some carbs have sneaked in. Also, not all cheeses are strictly vegetarian because animal rennet is used in the manufacturing. There are quite a few recipes here using Parmesan, and a proper Italian *Parmigiano Reggiano* will have been made using animal rennet. There are some very good vegetarian Parmesan substitutes out there, so please seek them out. When buying any of the cheeses used in this book, please check the label to make sure it's vegetarian if that is a concern for you.

FIBER

One criticism by nutritionists of low-carb diets is the lack of fiber, which is essential to keep the digestive system on track. A vegetarian low-carb diet is safe from this worry, provided you eat plenty of the permitted low-carb vegetables used in this book.

SUGAR

This is the BIG no-no. All sugars, refined or not, are pure carbohydrate and will send your insulin levels soaring and throw your metabolism off kilter if you are maintaining a strict low-carb lifestyle. Low-calorie sweetener is the low-carb alternative. All recipes in this book that contain a sweet element were developed using Splenda® brand granulated sweetener, a sucralose-based product (see www.splenda.com for more information). Canderel Yellow® Granular is another suitable sucralose product. These sweeteners are derived from sugar but have virtually no calories or carbs and do not affect insulin levels. Unlike some sweeteners, they are suitable for cooking and will stay sweet when subjected to heat. They do have a bit of an aftertaste, but seem to taste more authentic when an acidic element such as lemon is introduced, as is true of some other sugar-free sweeteners. Have you noticed how much a squeeze of lemon improves the flavor of diet cola?

If you prefer not to use a sucralose product, you could try an alternative such as xylitol, or a stevia-based sweetener, such as Truvia® or Canderel Green®. Please bear in mind that use of these sweeteners might require changing the quantities used in the recipes, so check the product packaging and the recommendations on their websites.

In the Sweet Things chapter, I have used highest-quality diabetic chocolate for some recipes. This chocolate is sweetened with sugar alcohols, such as maltitol or sorbitol. Look for it online, in health-food stores, and pharmacies.

FAT

Fats, like carbs, are often misunderstood, and it is a blanket generalization to assume they are all bad. There are good fats and bad fats. Plant sources are good fats. Good fats, from plant sources (monounsaturated, polyunsaturated, and omegas) are an essential part of our diet and actually lower cholesterol. Animal fats, including eggs and dairy, were once considered bad fats, but in fact they are good for health. They do not raise cholesterol and clog the arteries as once thought. The worst offenders are trans fats—highly processed solid fats used in certain margarines and processed foods—which have been proven dangerous. Always check labels on processed foods and avoid anything that contains the word "hydrogenated" in the ingredients.

Fat contains twice the calories of carbs, so it seems logical that if you cut out fat, you'll lose calories and hence weight, but this is a misconception that led to an obsession with avoiding fat. As with carbs, the trick is actually to avoid the bad and enjoy the good, and as with all things, in moderation.

CARBS

Not all carbs are your enemy. There are evil carbs and angelic ones. Generally, the bad guys are the white, refined carbs, including white bread, white pasta, potatoes, white rice, and white sugar. These are the foods that will give you a surge of energy followed by a crash and a new wave of hunger pangs, potentially leading to progressive snacking, bingeing, and weight gain. To make matters worse, they have few nutritional benefits otherwise. The good guys are the unrefined carbs, including whole grains, such as brown rice, whole-wheat pasta, fruits, and vegetables. These are essential for a healthy diet. Grain products are not included in this book because I strove to keep each recipe under 10 g of carbs.

If you are looking for substitutes for pasta, noodles, and rice, there are some fantastic carb-free and low-carb substitutes available online and in specialty suppliers. Traditional Asian shirataki noodles are virtually carb-free and calorie-free and are a natural product made from a root called konjac. There are several types of noodles and "rice" made from konjac. Follow the package directions carefully when cooking.

GLUTEN

I have avoided all wheat and most grain products in creating the recipes for this book so, by default, every recipe is gluten-free. Obviously, if you are following a strict gluten-free diet, you should check the label on any manufactured ingredients to be sure they are suitable for you. There are a number of recipes that use soy sauce, so make sure you choose a gluten-free version, such as a Japanese tamari (shoyu is made using wheat and soy).

THE LAST WORD...WATER

Drinking water is one of the most important parts of weight loss and daily function generally. It flushes out toxins, gives a feeling of fullness, speeds up weight loss, and keeps every cell in your body functioning properly. Keep a bottle with you at all times and drink at least eight 8-ounce glasses a day.

GUIDELINES FOR A HEALTHY LOW-CARB DIET

- Eat the right carbs: plenty of permitted vegetables and wholefoods. Avoid refined carbs and sugars.

- Increase your lean-protein intake. At each meal, make the protein portion the larger one, the carb portion the smaller one, and always include fresh vegetables.

- As well as eating your greens, take a multivitamin and mineral supplement.

- Don't worry about saturated fat. It's trans fats and sugars that you need to avoid.

- Relax and enjoy cooking. Bon appétit!

the low-carb kitchen

If you are committing to a low-carb diet, then it's a good idea to have a "carb cull" and remove all temptation from your kitchen. Gather all high-carb foods and give them to friends or donate them to charity. If other members of your household are still eating carbs, then designate a "carb cupboard" for them and stash their ingredients away. Out of sight, out of mind.

Outlined here is a selection of foods that are acceptable on the diet. Keeping a well stocked kitchen will make the diet easy to follow and the cooking more enjoyable. In the case of fresh produce, always try to buy whatever is in season close to the time you want to cook it, and buy organic where possible.

* = READ THE LABEL
Products containing sugar, corn syrup, modified starch, and anything hydrogenated should be avoided.

DAIRY

- Cheese, cream cheese
- Cottage cheese
- Ricotta, mascarpone
- Butter
- Crème fraîche/sour cream, regular or reduced fat
- Whipping cream
- Semiskim milk
- Thick/Greek/low-fat yogurt

EGGS

- Buy organic
- Store in the fridge

TOFU

- Firm—store in the fridge. Unused portions can be stored, covered in fresh water, in the fridge for up to 3 days, changing the water daily. Can be frozen
- Silken—usually sold in a long-life carton; suitable for smoothies and desserts. Unused portions should be stored in the fridge and used within 24 hours
- Smoked—store in the fridge. Can be frozen
- Flavored*/marinated*—store in the fridge. Can be frozen

OTHER SOY/ VEGETARIAN PRODUCTS, DRIED, CHILLED, OR FROZEN

- Soy flour (defatted)—store in fridge
- Textured vegetable protein (TVP)*
- Quorn™ and Quorn™ products*
- Vegetarian hot dogs*, sausages*
- Bacon-flavor soy bits* and strips*
- Vegetarian deli meat, such as sliced "ham" and "chicken"*

NUTS/SEEDS

- All types. Store in airtight container in a cool place for a short period, or in the freezer for longer periods. Cashews are the only relatively high-carb nuts, but fine in moderation

SPICES

- All types. Store away from sunlight. Buy whole spices and grind fresh if possible. Check the label of spice mixtures, which might contain sugar

CONDIMENTS/ FLAVORINGS

- Sugar-free sweetener (recipes in this book have been developed using granulated Splenda®—see pp.9–10)
- Sea salt
- Almond extract*
- Pure vanilla extract*
- Tabasco® sauce
- Other chili sauces*
- Soy sauce (such as a gluten-free tamari), light and dark
- Mustard*, dry and prepared
- Mayonnaise*
- Peanut butter*
- Cooking wines: sherry, Madeira, Marsala

CANS/JARS

- Italian diced tomatoes
- Artichoke hearts/bottoms
- Pickled vegetables*
- Pickled chiles, such as jalapeños*
- Green and black olives
- Capers
- Roasted peppers*
- Water chestnuts
- Palm hearts
- Coconut milk/cream

- Pesto*
- Tapenade*

FRESH PRODUCE

- All green vegetables and salad
- Cauliflower
- Scallions, shallots, onions, garlic, leeks
- Eggplant
- Pumpkin
- Asparagus
- Zucchini
- Celeriac, rutabaga, turnips
- Bell peppers
- Mung bean sprouts and other sprouted seeds, such as alfalfa
- Avocados
- Cucumber
- Celery
- Fennel
- Green beans, snow peas, sugar snap peas
- Mushrooms of all types, fresh and dried
- Radishes
- Tomatoes
- Red and green chiles
- Ginger
- Lemons, limes
- Fresh berries, melon

DRINKS

- Natural mineral water—drink eight 8-ounce glasses a day
- Herbal tea (sweetened with sugar-free sweetener only)
- Tea/coffee
- White wine
- Vodka and some other spirits*
- Sugar-free mixers/carbonated drinks*

01:
BREAK FAST

A high-protein fuel injection at breakfast will propel you into a sustained orbit until lunchtime. Breakfast is the key to keeping hunger at bay throughout the day. Don't miss it.

Blueberry Almond Griddle Cakes

These Southern-style pancakes are sweet, nutty, and laced with bursting blueberries. Don't be confused by putting the berries in the pan before the batter—it is the best way to distribute and cook them evenly, rather than mixing them into the batter.

⅓ cup soy flour

¼ cup ground almonds

2 tablespoons sweetener

½ teaspoon baking powder

Pinch of salt

2 eggs

3½ tablespoons heavy cream

2 teaspoons butter

½ cup blueberries

2 tablespoons Greek yogurt,
    to serve (optional)

Makes 12/Serves 4

Preheat the oven to 250°F for keeping the griddle cakes warm. Place the soy flour, almonds, sweetener, baking powder, salt, eggs, and heavy cream in a blender and process until smooth.

Heat a large nonstick skillet or griddle over low to medium heat and add 1 teaspoon of the butter. Tilt the pan to coat the surface with the melted butter. Allowing 4–5 blueberries for each griddle cake, place a cluster of berries in three places in the pan and carefully pour the batter over them to make three griddle cakes about 2½ inches in diameter. Cook until risen, golden on the undersides, and dry around the edges, then flip over and cook the other side until golden. Keep warm in the oven while you cook the remaining griddle cakes, adding the remaining butter between batches. Serve warm with the yogurt, if you like.

Per serving
Carbs: 5 g protein: 11 g calories: 267 fiber: 3 g fat: 23 g (saturated fat: 8 g)

Chocolate Breakfast Shake

Chocolate for breakfast? Why not? Pure unsweetened cocoa powder contains beneficial antioxidants, you get a little probiotic culture from the yogurt, and tofu is loaded with protein. So, this delicious sugar-free shake is healthier than you might think.

5 ounces silken tofu

2 tablespoons Greek yogurt

scant cup water

2 tablespoons pure unsweetened
   cocoa powder

½ teaspoon pure vanilla essence

large pinch ground cinnamon,
   or to taste

3 tablespoons sweetener, or to taste

Serves 2

Place all ingredients in a blender and process until smooth. Taste for sweetness and add more sweetener to suit. For a thicker texture, use less water in the mixture.

Per serving
Carbs: 2 g protein: 7 g calories: 78 fiber: 0.5 g fat: 5 g (saturated fat: 1.5 g)

Melon Berry Power Smoothie

Blast off with this fruity, high-protein concoction—guaranteed to give your day a kickstart.

5 ounces silken tofu

½ cup cantaloupe melon chunks

scant ½ cup raspberries

3 tablespoons ground almonds

½ teaspoon almond extract

1 teaspoon mixed spice, or to taste

2 tablespoons sweetener, or to taste

5 tablespoons water

Serves 2

Place all ingredients in a blender and process until smooth. Taste for sweetness and add more sweetener to suit.

Per serving
Carbs: 7.5 g protein: 11 g calories: 217 fiber: 3 g fat: 16 g (saturated fat: 1.5 g)

Turkish Breakfast

A satisfying, summery collection of tasty morsels, this traditional breakfast brings the essence of the Mediterranean to your table first thing in the morning. Boiling the egg in this fashion gives it a "buttery" yolk— not too runny, not too powdery, but just right. This recipe serves per person, but you can multiply it any number of times. Strong black tea is the customary accompaniment.

1 organic egg

1-ounce slice feta cheese, crumbled
    into chunks

1 medium tomato, quartered

½ cup cucumber chunks

¼ cup good-quality black olives, such
    as Kalamata

1 tablespoon olive oil

½ teaspoon dried oregano,
    or 1 teaspoon fresh oregano

Salt and freshly ground black pepper

Serves 1

Place the egg in a pan and cover with cold water. Bring to a boil, then simmer for 7 minutes. Drain and rinse under cold water until cool. Crack and remove the shell and cut the egg in half—it should be set but the yolk should still be buttery.

Toss the remaining ingredients in a bowl, place on a plate, and top with the egg. Drizzle with the olive oil, scatter with oregano, and season with salt and pepper to serve.

Per serving
Carbs: 3 g protein: 13 g calories: 318 fiber: 2.5 g fat: 28 g (saturated fat: 8 g)

Japanese Omelet

Making this light, multilayered, rolled omelet might take a little practice, but the result is mightily impressive. While you are making it, don't worry if some of the layers break up slightly because they will repair themselves in the final step. The added mushrooms give the omelet a rich nutty flavor, but they are not essential. Can be made up to 1 hour in advance.

6 shiitake mushrooms

1 tablespoon vegetable oil

8 organic eggs

½ cup Vegetable Stock
(see p.162)

1 tablespoon light soy sauce

Serves 4

Discard the stems of the shiitake mushrooms and slice very thinly. Heat a large nonstick skillet over medium heat and add 2 teaspoons of the oil. Cook the mushrooms until they are tinged with gold, then drain on paper towels.

Beat the eggs with remaining ingredients in a pitcher. Reheat the pan with the remaining oil over low to medium heat and pour in just enough of the egg mixture to cover the bottom, swirling to coat. Scatter with a few mushroom slices. Cook until barely set but not dry, then loosen the edges with a spatula and fold over three or four times to one side of the pan. (It may help to use a wide slotted lifter, two spatulas, or chopsticks.)

Pour in a little more egg mixture, swirl to coat the pan, and allow the mixture to attach itself to the cooked omelet. Scatter with a few mushroom slices and cook until barely set. Loosen as before and roll up in the opposite direction, starting with the previously cooked omelet.

Pour in more egg and mushrooms, and repeat the process, back and forth, until the egg mixture is used up and you have a long "sausage" of omelet.

Spread out a large piece of foil. Slide the omelet into the middle and roll up in the foil, gently forming it into a firm brick shape. Keep warm until ready to serve, then unwrap on a board and cut into eight slices or four pieces.

Per serving
Carbs: 0.3g protein: 16 g calories: 216 fiber: 0.5 g fat: 17 g (saturated fat: 4 g)

Kerala-Style Eggs

My cooking is heavily influenced by India, partly because it's a vegetarian's paradise, but also because I have spent some time in Kerala, the southernmost state. This is my version of one of my favorite Keralan breakfast dishes. Frying the black or brown mustard seeds first gives the egg dish an authentic and wonderful nuttiness, but if you can't find them, don't worry—just leave out that step, and start by frying the onions, chiles, etc.

4 organic eggs

1 tablespoons sunflower oil

½ teaspoon black or brown mustard
    seeds

2 scallions, chopped

1 fresh red chile, sliced or chopped
    (seeded if large)

½ teaspoon finely grated fresh ginger

½ teaspoon ground turmeric

1 medium-sized tomato, diced

Handful of fresh cilantro, chopped

Salt and freshly ground black pepper

2 teaspoons Greek yogurt, to serve
    (optional)

Serves 2

Beat the eggs in a bowl with a large pinch of salt until frothy. Set aside.

Heat a nonstick skillet over medium to high heat and pour in the oil. Add the mustard seeds and when they start to pop, lower the heat. Add the scallions and chile and cook for about 1 minute, until fragrant. Add the ginger and turmeric and stir, then add tomatoes and cook for about 1 minute more.

When the tomatoes are heated through, pour in the eggs. When the eggs have set on the bottom of the pan, start stirring gently with a folding motion. Cook until nearly set, then stir in the cilantro and remove from the heat. Serve on warm plates with a spoonful of yogurt and plenty of freshly ground black pepper.

Per serving
Carbs: 2.5 g protein: 16 g calories: 240 fiber: 0.7 g fat: 19 g (saturated fat: 5 g)

Three-Minute Egg
and Mushroom Bowl

The microwave is brilliant for cooking vegetables with a high water content, such as mushrooms. This recipe is so speedy it might well be the fastest low-carb breakfast in the West! The recipe is for one, but of course it can be multiplied—although it's best to cook each portion individually.

1 large flat portobello mushroom,
    stem removed
1 teaspoon truffle oil or olive oil
1 egg
Sea salt and freshly ground
    black pepper
1 ounce extra sharp cheddar or other
    strong, tangy cheese, cut into
    2 slices
1 teaspoon bacon-flavored soy bits
    (optional)

Serves 1

Choose a microwave-safe bowl that is just wide enough to accommodate the mushroom cap but not much bigger. Place the mushroom cap, gill-side up, in the bowl. Drizzle the truffle oil or olive oil over the gills and season with salt and pepper. (You could also add a little minced garlic or some chopped fresh herbs at this stage.)

Break the egg into the mushroom. Season lightly and prick the yolk with a fork to prevent it from exploding. Cross the cheese slices on top. Scatter with the bacon-flavored soy bits, if using.

Microwave on high for 1 minute, then check. The cooking time is variable (1½–2 minutes), depending on the moisture content and size of the mushroom, the size of the egg, the power of the microwave, etc. It's best to judge by the cheese, which should be bubbly and slightly crisp. The egg white should be completely set.

Per serving
Carbs: 0.2 g protein: 15 g calories: 223 fiber: 0.4 g fat: 18 g (saturated fat: 8 g)

Eggs Florentine
with Broiled Mushrooms

Juicy, truffle-scented portobello mushrooms replace English muffins in this timeless classic— a fabulous brunch dish. A little multitasking is required, but it's worth it. Warm plates are absolutely essential for serving—place them in the bottom of the oven while the mushrooms are cooking. If you don't have a broiler, simply roast the mushrooms at 400°F instead.

4 large, flat portobello mushrooms

2 tablespoons olive oil

2 teaspoons truffle oil (optional)

4 organic eggs

14 ounces young spinach leaves

1 quantity Blender Hollandaise
   (see p.164)

Salt and freshly ground black pepper

Serves 4

First, cook the mushrooms. Preheat the broiler to its highest setting. Snap the stems out of the mushrooms and discard. Brush the caps with olive oil and place, gill-side up, on a baking pan. Season with salt and pepper, and drizzle the remaining olive oil and truffle oil, if using, over the gills. Place under the broiler for about 8 minutes, until juicy. Keep warm.

Meanwhile, poach the eggs. Bring a ¾-inch depth of water to a boil in a large, nonstick skillet. Lower the heat to a gentle simmer. One at a time, carefully break each egg into a cup, then slide it into the water. Simmer for 2 minutes. Turn off the heat and leave the eggs to stand in the water for 10 minutes for slightly runny yolks. If you prefer a well done yolk, return the pan to the heat for 1–2 minutes, or until cooked to your liking. Place a couple of layers of paper towel on a plate. Remove the eggs from the pan with a slotted spoon and dry briefly on the paper. Keep warm.

Place the spinach in a large, heatproof bowl and add boiling water. Stir until wilted, then drain thoroughly in a strainer or colander, pressing out the excess moisture with a potato masher. Keep the spinach warm while you make the hollandaise sauce, which ideally should be made just before serving, but can also be made ahead and reheated.

Place a broiled mushroom cap on each of four warm plates. Top with some spinach, then a poached egg. Finish with warm hollandaise sauce and a good grinding of black pepper.

Per serving
Carbs: 2.5 g protein: 14 g calories: 499 fiber: 3 g fat: 48 g (saturated fat: 23 g)

Cottage Cheese Scramble

This recipe produces the tastiest and easiest scrambled eggs, all done in just three minutes. The wonderful cottage cheese imparts a richness and texture that makes toast just seem irrelevant. You can supplement this breakfast with a vegetarian sausage or two (low-carb ones, of course—always read the label), cooked in the microwave for speed and ease.

4 eggs

¼ cup cottage cheese, drained

Sea salt and freshly ground
   black pepper

1 teaspoon butter

Serves 2

Beat together the eggs, cottage cheese, and seasoning in a bowl. Heat a nonstick skillet over low heat and add the butter. Pour in the eggs. Cook until the underside is just set, then stir gently until the whole mixture is just set. Serve immediately.

(This can also be cooked in a microwave: Place the egg mixture in a microwave-safe bowl and add the butter. Cook on high power for 1 minute, then stir. Cook for a further 1–2 minutes, stopping and stirring with a clean fork every minute until cooked to your liking.)

Per serving
Carbs: 1 g protein: 19 g calories: 228 fiber: 0 g fat: 17 g (saturated fat: 6 g)

Cottage Cheese Pancakes with Berry Purée

A short stack of these classic American-style pancakes makes a filling breakfast. They can also be frozen (after cooking and cooling), then reheated in a toaster straight from the freezer.

2 tablespoons soy flour

1 teaspoon sweetener

½ cup cottage cheese

2 eggs, beaten

½ teaspoon baking powder

Generous pinch of sea salt

1 teaspoon sunflower oil

Raspberry Purée (see p.165),
    to serve

Serves 2

Preheat the oven to about 250°F to keep the pancakes warm once cooked.

Beat together the flour, sweetener, cottage cheese, eggs, baking powder, and salt until well mixed, making sure there are no lumps of flour.

Place a large nonstick skillet over medium heat and add the oil. Cook tablespoonfuls of the mixture in batches. When golden underneath, flip the pancakes over carefully—they remain slightly runnier on top than standard pancakes. Cook the second side, then remove to a plate and keep warm while you cook another batch.

Serve warm with Raspberry Purée (see p.165) spooned on top of each pancake.

Per serving
Carbs: 5 g protein: 17 g calories: 194 fiber: 2 g fat: 12 g (saturated fat: 3.5 g)

Almond Muffins

These protein-packed muffins are easy to grab and eat on busy mornings. This recipe makes a large batch, but they keep well for up to four days in an airtight container or can be frozen. Alternatively, you can divide the recipe in half or into thirds, if you want to make fewer.

For the dry mixture
2¼ cups soy flour
1½ cups ground almonds
3 teaspoons baking powder
1 cup less 1 tablespoon sweetener
1 teaspoon salt

For the wet mixture
6 eggs, beaten
½ cup reduced fat crème fraîche or
    sour cream
1 tablespoon vanilla extract
1½ teaspoons almond extract
½ cup sunflower oil

To decorate and serve
36 blanched almonds
butter

Makes 12

Preheat oven to 350°F. Grease a 12-cup muffin pan or line with paper baking cups and set aside.

Combine all the dry ingredients in a bowl, smoothing out any lumps in the flour.

Beat together all the wet ingredients in another bowl. Thoroughly combine the two mixtures, but do not overmix.

Pour the batter into the prepared muffin pan. Place 3 blanched almonds on top of each. Bake for 20–30 minutes, or until risen, golden, and firm. Rest for 5 minutes in the pan, then turn out onto a wire rack to cool. Serve warm, with butter for spreading.

Per serving
Carbs: 6 g protein: 14 g calories: 298 fiber: 3 g fat: 24 g (saturated fat: 4 g)

02:
SMALL COURSES

These little dishes can be mixed and matched with other recipes from this book for a table full of treats, the prelude to a main course, instalments in a multicourse feast, or served as a single light meal.

Fragrant Coconut Broth

Here's the closest thing you can possibly get to fresh coconut milk—an easy method of reconstituting dried coconut, then pressing out the milk. You'll be amazed how light and refreshing it tastes. If you are short of time, use a standard 14-ounce can of coconut milk plus 2¼ cups water or vegetable stock instead.

2¾ cups desiccated coconut
    (unsweetened)
2 pints (4½ cups) boiling water
1½-inch piece of fresh ginger, peeled
2 lemongrass stalks, trimmed
2 tablespoons light soy sauce,
    or to taste
1 tablespoon sweetener
½ cup button mushrooms, sliced
scant cup broccoli florets, chopped
1 tablespoon lemon juice
Handful of fresh cilantro leaves
    (optional)

Serves 4

Place the coconut in a bowl, add the boiling water, and let cool. When cold, purée with an electric hand-held mixer or stand blender, then push through a strainer, squeezing out as much coconut milk as possible; there should be just under 4¼ cups.

Slice the ginger and lemongrass—doing this now will maximize the flavor (as opposed to slicing ahead of time). Place in a pan with the coconut milk, soy sauce, and sweetener.

Bring to a boil, lower the heat, and simmer, stirring occasionally, for 10 minutes. Add the mushrooms and broccoli, return to a boil, and cook for 3 minutes. Ladle the broth into small bowls. Season each bowl with a little lemon juice, scatter with cilantro leaves (if using), and serve.

Per serving
Carbs: 5 g protein: 5 g calories: 388 fiber: 9 g fat: 39 g (saturated fat: 33 g)

Asian Wild Mushroom Broth

Dried mushrooms, such as shiitake, have a concentrated flavor that is released into this light and cleansing broth, giving it a rich, nutty undertone.

2 pints (4¼ cups) Vegetable Stock
(see p.162)
10 dried shiitake mushrooms
or other dried mushrooms,
(about ¼ ounce), rinsed
1 tablespoon sunflower oil
1 garlic clove, minced
¾-inch piece of fresh ginger, minced
3½ ounces tofu, finely diced
5 ounces fresh mixed wild or
cultivated exotic mushrooms (such
as enoki, shimeji, oyster, shiitake),
cut into bite-sized pieces
1 tablespoon dark soy sauce
¾ ounce salad cress, such as mustard
or shiso, or other sprouting seeds,
trimmed and cleaned

Serves 4

Place the stock and dried mushrooms in a saucepan and bring to a boil. Simmer for at least 15 minutes. (If the shiitake mushrooms seem a little large to eat, use a pair of scissors to snip them to size in the broth, once softened. Alternatively, lift them out with a slotted spoon, let them cool a little, then chop and return them to the broth.)

Meanwhile, heat a small skillet over medium heat and add the sunflower oil. Add garlic, ginger, and tofu, and stir-fry for about 2 minutes, until fragrant but not brown. Add the fresh mushrooms and stir-fry until soft and juicy. Add the soy sauce and remove from the heat.

Empty the contents of the skillet into the simmering stock. Bring back to a simmer for 5 minutes, then taste for seasoning. Ladle the soup into bowls, scatter with cress or sprouting seeds, and serve.

Per serving
Carbs: 8 g protein: 13 g calories: 141 fiber: 0.5 g fat: 7 g (saturated fat: 0.4 g)

Porcini Mushroom Soup with Thyme

Dried porcini mushrooms are a magical stock item with the power to transform the ordinary into something elegant. Cooking this velvety soup fills the house with delectable earthy aromas.

1 ounce dried porcini mushrooms

2¼ cups boiling Vegetable Stock (see p.162) or water

2 tablespoons olive oil

3 garlic cloves, crushed

1¼ pounds flat or other fresh mushrooms, coarsely chopped

1½ teaspoons salt

Bunch of fresh thyme, rinsed and tied together, or

1 teaspoon dried thyme

¾ cup Madeira, sherry, or Marsala

¼ cup reduced-fat crème fraîche or sour cream

¼ cup chopped parsley

Freshly ground black pepper

Serves 4

Rinse the porcini to remove any soil or grit, then place in a bowl and add the boiling stock or water. Leave for 20 minutes, then strain over a bowl, reserving the liquid. Coarsely chop the porcini.

Heat the olive oil in a pan over low to medium heat and add the garlic. Cook for just a few seconds, until it becomes fragrant, without letting it burn or color too much. Add the chopped mushrooms and porcini and season with the salt and plenty of pepper. Stir, then cover and cook, stirring occasionally, for about 10 minutes, or until the mushrooms have collapsed and are stewing in their juices.

Add the thyme and wine, then pour in the reserved mushroom soaking liquid through a fine strainer, to leave behind any extra grit that may have settled. Bring to a boil, then lower the heat to a simmer. Cook, uncovered, for 10 minutes. Cool briefly, then remove and discard the thyme bundle, if using, and purée the soup with a hand-held blender or in a food processor. Check the seasoning. The texture of the soup may vary depending on how juicy your mushrooms are; if it seems too thick, dilute with a little boiling water. Ladle into bowls and finish each with a tablespoon of crème fraîche or sour cream and chopped parsley.

Per serving
Carbs: 7 g protein: 4 g calories: 163 fiber: 1.5 g fat: 8 g (saturated fat: 2.5 g)

Egg Flower Soup

"Flower" in the title of this recipe refers to the appearance of the eggs, which resemble chrysanthemum petals as they cook in this delicious and healthy soup. The vegetables can be adapted according to what you have available—you can substitute spinach, watercress, asparagus, or zucchini, or add a little extra ginger or chile if you like.

1 tablespoon sunflower oil

¾ cup scallions, chopped

2 teaspoons sesame seeds

2 cups broccoli, chopped

1½ cups green cabbage,
    finely shredded

4¼ cups Vegetable Stock (see p.162)

1 tablespoon rice vinegar

1 teaspoon Chinese five-spice powder

3 organic eggs

2 tablespoons light soy sauce

1 tablespoon dry sherry

Sea salt and freshly ground
    black pepper

Serves 4

Place a pan over low to medium heat and add the oil. Add the scallions and sesame seeds and cook for about 2 minutes, or until the sesame seeds start to turn golden. Add the broccoli and cabbage (or green vegetables of your choice) and stir-fry for about 1 minute, or until bright green. Pour in the stock, season with pepper, and add the vinegar and five-spice powder. Bring to a boil.

Meanwhile, beat together the eggs, soy sauce, and sherry in a pitcher. While stirring the boiling soup rapidly and constantly, gradually pour in the egg mixture in a steady stream. The eggs should set immediately and the soup is ready to serve.

Carbs: 5 g protein: 9 g calories: 150 fiber: 2 g fat: 10 g (saturated fat: 2 g)

Smoky Eggplant Timbales

"Timbale" describes anything prepared in a small, round mold, either layered, as here, or solid, as in Red Pepper and Goat Cheese Timbales (see p.45). Choose plump eggplants with about the same circumference as the ramekins, but remember that they shrink a lot when cooked. The smoky pesto has a dazzling flavor, and can be used as a sauce in other dishes (see Spaghetti Squash with Smoked Chile Pesto, p.80).

2 large eggplants, about 1¼ pounds
    total
2 garlic cloves, sliced
Olive oil
4 ounces ricotta cheese
Salt and freshly ground black pepper
handful fresh basil leaves, to garnish

For the smoky pesto
1 teaspoon mild smoked paprika/
    pimentón
Bunch of fresh basil
heaping ¼ cup pine nuts
1 garlic clove
¼ cup grated fresh Parmesan cheese
3 tablespoons olive oil
Pinch of salt

Serves 4

Preheat the oven to 375°F.

Slice the eggplants into ½-inch thick disks. Mix the garlic with some olive oil in a cup and brush both sides of the disks. Place on a cookie sheet and scatter with the sliced garlic. Season with salt and pepper and bake for 20–30 minutes, or until soft and barely golden, then remove from the oven and let cool.

Make the pesto by processing all the ingredients in the food processor, adding the olive oil at the end. Taste for seasoning.

Brush 4 ramekins lightly with olive oil and place an eggplant disk in each. Place about a tablespoon of ricotta on top, a generous spoonful of pesto, then another eggplant disk. Continue with another layer of ricotta, pesto, then another eggplant disk. (Some pieces will be smaller than others, so use as many pieces of eggplant as necessary to fill the layer.)

Place the ramekins on a cookie sheet and bake for 15–20 minutes, or until sizzling. Cool briefly before inverting. To do this, place a plate upside down on top of each timbale and flip over. Remove the ramekin. Arrange basil leaves around the timbales and serve.

Per serving
Carbs: 5 g protein: 16 g calories: 541 fiber: 3 g fat: 51 g (saturated fat: 11 g)

Red Bell Pepper and Goat Cheese Timbales

Very elegant, coral-colored custards with a velvety texture, these can be eaten warm or cold with a small salad of young leaves. Team up with Avocado and Lemon Salad (see p.128) for an exquisite light lunch.

2 large red bell peppers, about
    11½ ounces trimmed weight,
    halved and cored
11 ounces mild, rindless soft
    goat cheese
1 garlic clove, crushed with salt in
    a mortar and pestle or with a
    garlic crusher
2 organic eggs
Generous grating of nutmeg
Butter, for greasing
Salt and freshly ground black pepper

Serves 4

Preheat the broiler or oven to its highest setting. Place the peppers, cut-side down, on a cookie sheet and broil or roast until the skins are blackened and charred all over. Transfer to a plastic bag, tie the top, and let sweat until cool, then peel off the skins.

Preheat the oven to 300°F. Place the roasted peppers, goat cheese, and garlic in a food processor and process until smooth. Season to taste. Add the eggs, one at a time, and a good grating of nutmeg. Process until absolutely smooth.

Generously grease four ramekins with butter and place in a roasting pan or ovenproof dish. Divide the mixture among the ramekins. Pour boiling water into the roasting pan or dish to come halfway up the sides of the ramekins. Bake for 30 minutes, or until firm. Remove from the oven and place the timbales on an oven rack to cool slightly, then turn out onto serving plates (to do this, place a plate upside down on top of each timbale and flip over). Remove the ramekin and serve.

Alternatively, let cool and serve chilled. To loosen from the ramekins, first stand in a bowl of hot water, then turn out.

Per serving
Carbs: 6 g protein: 21 g calories: 310 fiber: 1 g fat: 23 g (saturated fat: 14 g)

Portobello Mushrooms with Blue Cheese Custard

These juicy little numbers will appreciate the company of a crisp lettuce salad dressed with a little salt, white wine vinegar, and olive oil. Alternatively, turn them into a main course, paired up with Mashed Pumpkin and Turnips (see p.136).

6 large portobello mushrooms, about
　　¾ pound in total, stems removed
2 tablespoons olive oil
2 garlic cloves, minced
Sea salt and freshly ground
　　black pepper

For the blue cheese custard
3 ounces blue cheese, such as Stilton,
　　Roquefort, or Gorgonzola,
　　crumbled
¾ cup crème fraîche
2 organic egg yolks
1 tablespoon finely chopped fresh
　　tarragon leaves, plus extra
　　to garnish

Serves 6

Preheat the oven to 350°F. Brush the mushroom caps with half of the oil and place, gill-side up, in an ovenproof dish just large enough to hold them in a single layer. Scatter the gills with the minced garlic, drizzle with the remaining oil, and season with salt and pepper.

Beat together the cheese, crème fraîche, egg yolks, and tarragon with a pinch of salt. Spoon the mixture into the mushroom caps. Bake for about 20 minutes, or until the custard is set and bubbly and the mushrooms are soft. Scatter the mushrooms with more chopped tarragon and serve.

Per serving
Carbs: 1 g protein: 6 g calories: 207 fiber: 0.7 g fat: 20 g (saturated fat: 11 g)

Halloumi-Stuffed Bell Peppers

Here's one of my favorite ways to stuff bell peppers with no fuss. The recipe is very easy to multiply if you're feeding a crowd. These make a good partner for Roasted Eggplant with Dill Sauce (see p.133).

2 red bell peppers

4 basil leaves

1 large garlic clove, sliced

1 tablespoon pine nuts

2½ ounces halloumi cheese,
    cut into 4 slices or rough cubes
    (use feta if halloumi is unavailable)

¼ cup olive oil

Serves 2, or 4 as an
accompaniment

Preheat the oven to 400°F.

Cut the bell peppers in half from stem to base. Remove the seeds but leave the stems intact. Arrange the halves skin-side down, on a baking pan. Place a basil leaf in each pepper half, sprinkle with garlic and pine nuts, top with a slice of halloumi, and drizzle with a tablespoon of olive oil.

Bake for 20–30 minutes, or until the cheese is golden.

Per serving
Carbs: 4 g protein: 4 g calories: 195 fiber: 1.25 g fat: 17 g (saturated fat: 4.5 g)

Eggplant Rarebit

This is a filling, warming taste of cheese heaven, with roasted eggplant disks replacing the traditional toast.

1 large eggplant,
    sliced into 8 disks
1 tablespoon olive oil,
    plus extra for greasing
    and brushing
4 shallots or 1 medium onion,
    sliced
5 tablespoons white wine
3½ ounces extra sharp cheddar or
    other tangy cheese, grated
1 teaspoon dry mustard
2 organic eggs, beaten
Salt and freshly ground black pepper

Serves 4

Preheat the oven to 375°F.

Brush each eggplant disk all over with olive oil and place on a baking pan lined with nonstick paper. Season with salt and pepper, and bake for 20–30 minutes, or until softened and just turning golden.

Preheat the broiler to its highest setting. Alternatively, increase the oven temperature to 425°F.

Place a heavy pan over medium heat, add the olive oil, and cook the shallots or onion until softened. Turn the heat down as low as possible and add the wine, cheese, and mustard, stirring until the cheese melts. Add the beaten eggs and stir until the mixture thickens slightly, but remove from the heat before the eggs start to scramble. Spoon the mixture onto the baked eggplant disks, and broil or bake until puffed and patched with gold. Grind some black pepper onto the eggplant disks to serve.

Carbs: 3 g protein: 11 g calories: 200 fiber: 2 g fat: 15 g (saturated fat: 7 g)

Spiced Charred Eggplant

In this unusual cooking method, the eggplant steams in an aromatic broth that reduces
to a thick glaze, and finally becomes a slightly charred crust. You will need a large, nonstick
skillet with a lid for this. Just remember—don't stir. Serve with salad or cooked spinach.

2 medium-sized eggplants,
about 1¼ pounds,
cut into 1-inch dice

2 teaspoons coriander seeds,
lightly crushed

1 teaspoon cumin seeds

½ teaspoon ground turmeric

1 teaspoon salt, or to taste

1 large green chile, cut into 3–4 pieces

Large handful of fresh cilantro,
chopped

Freshly ground black pepper

1 cup water

3½ tablespoons butter, diced

Serves 4

Arrange the diced eggplant in an even layer in a large, nonstick skillet. Scatter evenly with
the coriander seeds, cumin seeds, turmeric, salt, chile, and chopped cilantro, and season
with pepper. Add the water and scatter with the diced butter. Cover the skillet, place on high
heat, and bring to a boil. Shake the pan a few times and lower the heat to a simmer. Cover
and cook without stirring, for about 20 minutes, checking occasionally that the water has not
dried out. If it has, add a little more.

After 20 minutes, the eggplant should be buttery soft and the liquid should have reduced to
a thick glaze. Do not stir. Remove the lid and increase the heat. Reduce the sauce until it just
starts to form a crust on the bottom of the pan. Remove from the heat.

Let stand for 2 minutes, then stir the crust through the eggplant. Serve hot or cold.

Carbs: 3.5 g protein: 1.5 g calories: 116 fiber: 3 g fat: 11 g (saturated fat: 7 g)

03:
LIGHT
LUNCH

Hearty soups and main-event salads feature here, perfect for a midday refueling. But don't just restrict them to lunch. Hot soups are perfect for winter nights, cool salads for balmy evenings.

Egg and Avocado Caesar

I call this "Caesar" because of the sharp, eggy dressing that gives it a resemblance to the classic salad. Avocado and olives make it a well rounded and substantial enough for lunch or supper.

6 organic eggs

¼ cup freshly grated Parmesan cheese

¼ cup white wine vinegar

1 teaspoon vegetarian Worcestershire
   sauce or light soy sauce

A small handful of fresh chives,
   snipped

Salt and freshly ground black pepper

¼ cup olive oil

2 ripe avocados

Juice of ½ lemon

2 hearts of romaine lettuce, torn

¾ cup good-quality black olives, such
   as Kalamata

Serves 4

Place the eggs in a small pan of cold water and bring to a boil. Boil for 7 minutes, then drain and rinse under cold water until cool. Crack the eggs, peel off the shell, and rinse again.

To make the dressing, place 2 peeled eggs in a bowl and mash well with a fork. Add the Parmesan, vinegar, Worcestershire or soy sauce, and chives. Season with salt and pepper and whisk thoroughly. Gradually whisk in the oil. (The dressing can also be blended with a stick blender or in a food processor if you want it completely smooth.)

Quarter the remaining eggs. Just before serving, peel the avocados, remove the seed, quarter the flesh, and sprinkle it lightly with lemon juice to prevent discoloration. Make a bed of lettuce on each plate and arrange the avocados, egg quarters, and olives on top. Drizzle the dressing onto the salad to serve.

Per serving
Carbs: 2 g protein: 20 g calories: 480 fiber: 3.5 g fat: 43 g (saturated fat: 11 g)

Curried Celeriac Soup
with Cilantro Oil

Thank heaven for celeriac, one of the few low-carb root vegetables. It gives this soup a creamy and satisfying texture. Ground almonds add richness and protein. Whole spices always produce the best flavor, but you can use ground spices instead if you're in a hurry. The cilantro oil is optional, but it makes the soup look and taste even more fabulous.

2 teaspoons coriander seeds

1 teaspoon cumin seeds

½ teaspoon dried red pepper flakes,
    or to taste

2 tablespoons butter

2 teaspoon ground turmeric

1 large onion, diced

3 garlic cloves, minced

1-inch piece of fresh ginger, chopped

¼ cup ground almonds

1¾ pounds celeriac, diced

5 cups Vegetable Stock
    (see p.162)

Salt and freshly ground black pepper

For the cilantro oil

1 small garlic clove

½ teaspoon coarse sea salt

Handful of cilantro leaves

¼ cup olive oil

¼ cup heavy cream, to serve

Serves 6

To make the soup, grind together the coriander seeds, cumin seeds, and dried red pepper flakes in a spice grinder or pound in a mortar with a pestle. Melt the butter in a large pan over low heat. Add the crushed spices and the turmeric and cook for about 1 minute, or until fragrant. Add the onion, cover, and cook for about 5 minutes, until translucent. Add the garlic, ginger, and almonds and cook for 1 minute. Add the celeriac and stock and bring to a boil. Simmer for 20 minutes, or until the celeriac is tender, then purée the soup with a stick blender or in a food processor until smooth. Season to taste with salt and pepper.

To make the cilantro oil, grind all the ingredients together in a spice grinder or food processor, or pound to a smooth paste using a mortar and pestle.

To serve, ladle the soup into bowls. Swirl a tablespoon each of the cilantro oil and the cream into each serving. Sesame and Black Pepper Crispbreads (see p.108) make a good accompaniment to this soup.

Per serving

Carbs: 6 g protein: 4.5 g calories: 237 fiber: 6 g fat: 21 g (saturated fat: 7 g)

Cauliflower, Coconut, and Cardamom Soup

A thick and substantial potage, where three Cs come together to form a dazzling combo. Two equally appealing textures can be achieved with this soup—chunky or smooth.

1 tablespoon sunflower oil

1¼-pound cauliflower, chopped

5 ounces zucchini, chopped

2 garlic cloves, chopped

3 scallions (white and
    clean green parts), chopped

Sea salt and freshly ground
    black pepper

½ teaspoon cardamom seed (from
    about 20 pods), ground or
    pounded in a mortar and pestle
    or spice grinder

A good grating of nutmeg

1 cup coconut milk

1½ cups Vegetable Stock
    (see p.162)

Serves 4

Place a pot with a lid over medium heat and add the oil. Add the cauliflower, zucchini, garlic, and scallions and sprinkle with the salt, pepper, cardamom seeds, and grated nutmeg. Stir, cover, and let sweat for about 10 minutes, stirring from time to time.

Pour in the coconut milk and stock, and bring to a boil. Simmer for 10 minutes, or until the cauliflower is meltingly tender. Cool slightly, then for a slightly chunky texture, use a potato masher to crush the soup. Alternatively, use a stick blender to purée until smooth.

Sesame and Black Pepper Crispbreads (see p.108) go well with this soup.

Per serving
Carbs: 8 g protein: 8 g calories: 192 fiber: 3 g fat: 15 g (saturated fat: 6 g)

Chinese-Spice Tofu and Baby Leaf Salad

Tofu just needs a little loving attention to give it life. This simple treatment gives it loads of flavor, a light, crisp texture on the outside, and a creamy interior.

1¼ pounds fresh firm tofu

¼ cup sunflower oil

6 scallions, sliced

4 garlic cloves, sliced

1½-inch piece of fresh ginger, grated

2 teaspoons Chinese five-spice
   powder

Salt

¼ cup dark soy sauce

2 tablespoons rice vinegar

2 tablespoons sweetener

About 5 cups baby leaf salad

Serves 4

Drain the tofu and wrap in paper towels. Set aside while you prepare the remaining ingredients.

When you are ready to cook, cut the tofu into 1-inch cubes. Heat the oil in a large, nonstick skillet over medium heat and add the tofu, scallions, garlic, ginger, five-spice powder, and a pinch of salt. Stir-fry for about 3 minutes, or until the tofu is light gold in color.

Add the soy sauce, vinegar, and sweetener. Heat through, then remove the pan from the stove. Transfer the mixture to a bowl and let cool.

Toss the cooled tofu mixture through the baby leaves and serve immediately.

Per serving
Carbs: 3 g protein: 12 g calories: 210 fiber: 0.7 g fat: 17 g (saturated fat: 2 g)

Tofu, Mint, and Palm Heart Salad with Hot and Spicy Dressing

Mint, ginger, garlic, chile, and toasted sesame seeds harmonize in this many-textured, clean-tasting salad. If palm hearts are not available, use canned water chestnuts.

9 ounces fresh firm tofu, drained, patted dry, and cut into ¾-inch cubes

1 quantity Sweet Chili Sauce (see p.166), made with green chiles

2 tablespoons sesame seeds

2 teaspoons sesame oil

8 Chinese cabbage leaves, lower halves shredded, top halves left intact

Small bunch of fresh mint, leaves stripped

14-ounce can palm hearts, drained and sliced diagonally

1-inch piece of fresh ginger, cut into slivers

Serves 4

Place the tofu in a shallow dish and cover with the chili sauce. Let marinate at room temperature for 30 minutes or for longer in the refrigerator.

Heat a dry skillet over medium heat and add sesame seeds. Cook, stirring occasionally, until golden and popping. Transfer to a small bowl and let cool.

Drain the tofu, reserving the sauce. Mix the sauce with the sesame oil, beating well.

To assemble the salad, arrange two Chinese cabbage leaf tops on each of four plates. Mix together the shredded leaves, mint, sliced palm hearts, and ginger slivers and divide among the plates. Arrange the marinated tofu on top and scatter with toasted sesame seeds. Drizzle each serving with dressing to serve.

Per serving
Carbs: 4 g protein: 8.5 g calories: 135 fiber: 1 g fat: 8 g (saturated fat: 1 g)

Cyprus Salad

Resembling its sister the Greek salad (also a low-carb choice), this salad uses Cyprus's unique cheese, halloumi, instead of feta. If you can't find halloumi, try slicing feta in the same way and broiling until golden on top.

1¾ cups broccoli florets

1 cup cucumber chunks

3 celery sticks, trimmed and chopped
into chunks

1 green bell pepper, cored and
chopped into chunks

1 red bell pepper, cored and chopped
into chunks

heaping ¼ cup good-quality black
olives, such as Kalamata

Handful of flat-leaf parsley, chopped

Handful of mint leaves, chopped

9 ounces halloumi cheese, sliced across
the narrow end into 8 slices

Juice of ½ a lemon

For the dressing

½ small red onion, chopped

2 tablespoons fresh lemon juice

1 teaspoon fresh or dried thyme

Sea salt and freshly ground
black pepper

¼ cup extra virgin olive oil

Serves 4

First make the dressing. Mix together the onion, lemon juice, and thyme, and season with sea salt and pepper. Whisk in the olive oil, then taste and adjust the seasoning if necessary. Set aside to let the flavors mingle while you prepare the rest of the salad.

Boil, microwave, or steam the broccoli florets for 3 minutes, or until just tender. Refresh under cold running water, drain, and pat dry.

Mix together the broccoli, cucumber, celery, bell peppers, olives, and herbs in a bowl.

When you are ready to serve, heat a large, nonstick skillet over medium heat. Do not add oil. Arrange the halloumi slices in the pan. Cook until golden underneath, then turn them over and cook the other side. Meanwhile, stir the dressing through the salad and spoon onto plates.

As soon as the halloumi is golden, squeeze the lemon juice onto it in the hot pan and remove from the heat. Arrange the halloumi on top of the salad and serve immediately.

Per serving
Carbs: 8 g protein: 12 g calories: 311 fiber: 3 g fat: 25 g (saturated fat: 10 g)

Warm Exotic Mushroom Salad

I was lucky enough to be asked to present a short documentary for UKTV Food about a mushroom farm in Kent, in southeastern England. The farmer, Nigel Baddeley, grows exotic varieties from Japan in England, such as shimeji, nameko, and eringii mushrooms, all of which have a unique, nutty flavor. I created this recipe with the produce he gave me, but you could use any combination of wild or cultivated types, especially shiitake and oyster mushrooms.

2 tablespoons butter

2 garlic cloves, minced

11 ounces mixed wild and
    cultivated mushrooms,
    sliced if large

1 teaspoon fresh thyme leaves

½ cup Madeira wine

heaping ¼ cup mascarpone cheese

2 Little Gem or leaf lettuces

Sea salt and freshly ground
    black pepper

Serves 4

Melt the butter in a wide skillet over low heat and cook the garlic until fragrant. Add the mushrooms, season with salt and pepper, and cook gently until softened. Add the thyme and Madeira, and cook for a further 2 minutes. Stir in mascarpone and cook until it coats the mushrooms. Remove the pan from the heat and let cool briefly.

Arrange the lettuce leaves on plates and spoon the warm mushroom mixture onto them. Serve immediately.

Per serving

Carbs: 1 g protein: 2 g calories: 171 fiber: 1 g fat: 14 g (saturated fat: 9 g)

Warm Poached Egg Salad
with Tarragon Vinaigrette

My good friend Jennifer Joyce has kindly let me use this recipe from her gorgeous book *The Well-Dressed Salad*. This sophisticated salad is fully appreciated, she insists, "with a glass of chilled white Burgundy." I couldn't agree more—and only 1 g carbohydrate per glass!

4 organic eggs

7 ounces green beans, trimmed

1 tablespoon olive oil

Salt

For the dressing

2 teaspoons Dijon mustard

1 teaspoon red wine vinegar

½ teaspoon sea salt

Freshly ground black pepper

¾ cup olive oil

1 tablespoon capers, rinsed and
 chopped

1 tablespoon finely chopped flat-leaf
 parsley

Leaves from 2 tarragon sprigs,
 chopped

1 tablespoon minced shallot

Serves 4

First, poach the eggs. Bring a ¾-inch depth of water to a boil in a large, nonstick skillet. Reduce the heat to a low simmer. One at a time, carefully break each egg into a cup, then slide it into the water. Simmer for 2 minutes. Turn off the heat and let the eggs stand in the water for 10 minutes. They will then be perfectly cooked if you like the yolk slightly runny. If you prefer your yoke well done, put the pan back on the heat for 1–2 minutes, or until cooked to your liking. Place a couple of layers of paper towel on a plate. Remove the eggs from the pan with a slotted spoon and dry briefly on the paper. Keep warm if necessary.

Meanwhile, cook the beans and make the dressing. Bring a small pan of salted water to a boil. Blanch the beans for about 2 minutes, or until tender but still firm. Drain and cool under cold running water or plunge into ice-cold water to stop the cooking process.

To make the dressing, whisk together the mustard, vinegar, salt, and pepper to taste in a small bowl. Gradually whisk in the oil to emulsify. Stir in the capers, herbs, and shallot.

Return the beans to the dry pan and add the olive oil. Warm through on medium heat. Arrange the warm beans on individual serving plates, place an egg on top, and drizzle with the dressing to serve.

Per serving
Carbs: 4 g protein: 9 g calories: 436 fiber: 1.5 g fat: 42 g (saturated fat: 7 g)

Teriyaki Tofu
with Roasted Broccoli

Teriyaki is a rich and powerful Japanese ingredient that brings out the best in tofu, and broccoli loves its company as well. Serve this with a few slices of cool cucumber to balance the salty-sweet flavor.

½ cup dark soy sauce

scant cup dry sherry

½-inch piece of fresh ginger,
  finely grated

7 ounces tofu, patted dry and
  cut into 2 triangles

4 teaspoons sunflower oil

3¼ cups broccoli florets

Cucumber slices, to serve (optional)

Serves 2

Preheat the oven to 400°F. Place the soy sauce, sherry, and ginger in a small skillet and bring to a boil. Add the tofu and simmer for 5 minutes, then turn the tofu over and simmer for a further 5 minutes. Carefully lift the tofu from the sauce and place in a lightly oiled ovenproof dish. Reserve the sauce. Brush the top and sides of the tofu with 2 teaspoons of the oil.

Place the broccoli in a bowl, add the remaining oil, and toss to coat. Arrange the broccoli around the tofu. Pour the reserved sauce onto the broccoli and tofu. Roast for 25 minutes, or until the broccoli is cooked and slightly crisp. Serve hot with cucumber slices, if you like.

Per serving
Carbs: 1.7g protein: 7 g calories: 116 fiber: 2 g fat: 9 g (saturated fat: 1 g)

Spanish Tortilla
with Zucchini and Manchego

Choose a smallish, reliable nonstick skillet for the tortilla, ideally about 10 inches in diameter, with a heatproof handle that will be safe under the broiler. This may seem too small for the initial frying of the zucchini, but they do shrink considerably.

1 pound 10 ounces zucchini, thinly
    sliced
2 tablespoons olive oil
3 organic eggs
Sea salt and freshly ground
    black pepper
3½ ounces Manchego, feta, or other
    tangy cheese, cut into small dice

Serves 6

Heat a small, nonstick skillet over medium heat and add 1 tablespoon olive oil. Add the zucchini, season with a little salt and pepper, and cook, moving them around frequently, until soft and golden.

Preheat the broiler to its highest setting. Break the eggs into a large bowl and beat well with a little salt and pepper. Stir the zucchini and cheese into the eggs until the zucchini are well coated.

Return the pan to the heat and add the remaining olive oil. Scoop the egg mixture into the pan.

Cook, loosening the edges occasionally, until the tortilla is deep golden underneath and loose when you shake the pan. Place the pan under the broiler and cook until the egg is set throughout and the top is patched with gold. Carefully remove the tortilla from the pan and let cool. Serve warm or cold, cut into wedges.

Per serving
Carbs: 2.5 g protein: 10 g calories: 187 fiber: 1 g fat: 15 g (saturated fat: 5 g)

04:
MAIN COURSES

Feed your friends and family with these substantial dishes—tarts, gratins, stews, curries, and comfort food. Even those who are not on a low-carb diet can't fail to feel satisfied.

Vietnamese Asparagus Pancakes

This coconut batter is something that I dreamed up, but it fits deliciously into a Vietnamese-style pancake platter, with the essential cucumber and herb salad and hot-sweet sauce. If asparagus is out of season, try using lightly stir-fried beansprouts instead, or simply fill the pancakes with cucumber batons, cilantro, and mint sprigs.

2 bunches asparagus, 9 ounces total

4 teaspoons sunflower oil, divided

4 scallions, sliced

For the batter

¼ cup soy flour

3 organic eggs

½ cup canned coconut milk

½ teaspoon ground turmeric

Large pinch of salt

To serve

scant cup cucumber batons or slices

4 fresh cilantro sprigs

4 fresh mint sprigs

1 quantity Sweet Chili Sauce
   (see p.166)

Serves 4

Preheat the oven to 250°F. Steam the asparagus in a pan or in the microwave for 3 minutes, or until cooked to your liking. Keep warm in the preheated oven.

To make the batter, place the flour, eggs, coconut milk, turmeric, and salt in a blender and process until smooth. Heat a medium-sized nonstick skillet over medium heat and add 1 teaspoon oil. Add one-quarter of the batter in a thin layer and tilt the pan to coat the bottom. Scatter with one-quarter of the scallions before it sets. When golden underneath, flip the pancake over and cook until golden on the other side. Transfer to a plate and keep warm. Make three more pancakes in the same way, adding 1 teaspoon oil to the pan each time.

To serve, roll a pancake around half a bunch of asparagus, starting from the edge. Serve with cucumber, cilantro, and mint sprigs and a small bowl of sweet chili sauce.

Per serving

Carbs: 7 g protein: 14 g calories: 230 fiber: 3.6 g fat: 16 g (saturated fat: 2 g)

Arugula and Ricotta Cheesecake

This creamy, savory cheesecake is lightened with arugula and herbs. Serve with a crunchy leaf salad, or for a more full-on meal, with Braised Fennel and Bell Peppers (see p.132).

Butter, for greasing

heaping ½ cup walnut pieces

1 tablespoon olive oil

3 garlic cloves, chopped

3 scallions, chopped

4¼ cups arugula, coarsely chopped

3 tablespoons chopped fresh herbs,
    such as parsley, basil, and dill,
    plus extra to garnish

3 organic eggs

1¼ pounds ricotta cheese, drained

¼ cup freshly grated Parmesan cheese,
    plus extra shavings to garnish

Sea salt and freshly ground
    black pepper

Serves 6

Preheat the oven to 325°F. Generously butter an 8-inch cake pan with a removable bottom. Grind the walnut pieces to a powder in a food processor, then press them into the bottom and up the inside of the pan.

Set a skillet over low heat and pour in the olive oil. When the oil is hot, add the garlic and scallions and cook for 1 minute, or until fragrant. Add the arugula and herbs and stir for 1–2 minutes, or until the arugula is just wilted. Remove the skillet from the heat.

Put the eggs, ricotta, Parmesan, and the arugula mixture in a clean food processor, and season with salt and pepper. Process until evenly mixed. Pour into the prepared pan. Bake for about 45 minutes, or until golden and firm. Remove from the pan, cut into wedges, and serve warm.

Carbs: 3 g protein: 15 g calories: 293 fiber: 0.8 g fat: 24 g (saturated fat: 9 g)

Warm Eggplant Salad with Melting Camembert

Get ready for some guilt-free indulgence with this upmarket salad. Salting the eggplant disks will prevent them from absorbing too much of the oil.

2 medium eggplants,
    sliced into ½-inch disks

Olive oil

4 shallots, sliced

½ cup dry vermouth or white wine

1 tablespoon wine vinegar

2 radicchio or treviso, leaves torn

2½ cups firmly packed young spinach
    leaves

7 ounces chilled Camembert cheese,
    sliced into strips

½ cup walnut halves, lightly crushed

Handful of mint leaves, chopped

Salt and freshly ground black pepper

Serves 4

Spread out the eggplant disks in a colander and scatter with salt. Let drain for 30 minutes over the sink, then pat dry.

Heat a large skillet over medium heat and add ¼ cup olive oil. Cook the eggplant disks, in batches if necessary, until soft and golden, adding a little more oil if necessary. Remove the eggplant disks and add a drop more oil to the skillet, then cook the shallots until soft. Return all the eggplant disks to the pan and reheat.

Carefully pour in the vermouth or wine all at once—stand back because it may spatter at first. Season well with salt and pepper and cook, shaking the skillet gently, until the liquid has reduced by half. Add the vinegar to the skillet and shake. Cook for a further 2 minutes, while the juices thicken and caramelize, then remove the skillet from the heat. Preheat the broiler to its highest setting.

Meanwhile, make a bed of radicchio or treviso and young spinach leaves on a heatproof platter. Arrange the eggplant disks on top and drizzle with the pan juices. Place slices of Camembert on top and scatter with walnuts. Place the platter under the broiler until the cheese starts to melt. Finally, scatter with chopped mint to serve.

Per serving
Carbs: 5 g protein: 1 g calories: 162 fiber: 2 g fat: 13 g (saturated fat: 2 g)

Creamy Celeriac Gratin

**This makes a generous quantity, and believe me, you are going to want leftovers!
It also freezes well. Serve with Ruby Chard with Pine Nuts and Red Currants (see p.131).**

Butter, for greasing

3 garlic cloves

1 teaspoon coarse salt

1 large celeriac, 1½ pounds trimmed
   weight, peeled and grated

Generous grating of nutmeg

1¼ cups heavy cream

½ cup ground almonds

2 tablespoons chopped fresh parsley

¼ cup freshly grated Parmesan cheese

Salt and freshly ground black pepper

Serves 8

Preheat the oven to 400°F. Lightly butter a gratin dish.

Crush the garlic and salt in a mortar and pestle until smooth (alternatively use a garlic crusher).

Mix together the salted garlic, celeriac, nutmeg, and cream in a large bowl and season with pepper. Stir until well mixed—it helps to use clean hands to combine the mixture thoroughly. Spoon the mixture into the gratin dish and pack it down.

Mix together the almonds, parsley, and Parmesan and scatter the mixture evenly onto the gratin. Bake for about 40 minutes, or until soft and golden.

Per serving

Carbs: 3 g protein: 6 g calories: 271 fiber: 4 g fat: 26 g (saturated fat: 14 g)

Thai Hot and Sour Salad with Crispy Tofu

Here's a user-friendly version of the classic Thai salad known as "som tam." Low-carb turnip takes the place of green papaya and the tofu bumps up the protein quotient.

7 ounces firm tofu

Sunflower oil, for frying

For the dressing

2 red chiles, seeded if large

2 garlic cloves

¼ cup light soy sauce

¼ cup lime juice

¼ cup sweetener

For the salad

11-ounce turnip, grated

3½ ounces green beans, sliced lengthways

1 red bell pepper, cored and thinly sliced

4 scallions, sliced

2 handfuls of fresh mint leaves

scant ½ cup roasted peanuts, ground

Serves 4

First, drain the tofu and wrap in paper towels until ready to use.

Make the dressing by pounding all the ingredients in a heavy mortar or by processing them in a blender. Combine the turnip, beans, pepper, scallions, mint, and half the peanuts. Stir half the dressing through the salad.

Heat a shallow layer of oil in a skillet over high heat. Cut the tofu into 3-inch slices and fry, turning once, until golden all over. Drain on paper towels.

Spoon the salad onto plates and top with the tofu. Drizzle with the remaining dressing and scatter with the remaining peanuts to serve.

Per serving

Carbs: 10 g protein: 10 g calories: 159 fiber: 3.5 g fat: 9 g (saturated fat: 1.5 g)

Spinach and Ricotta Gnocchi with Sage Butter

These rich yet fluffy gnocchi make a proper Italian luxury meal. They can also be placed in an ovenproof dish after boiling, covered in grated cheese, and baked for a fabulous gratin.

2½ cups firmly packed young spinach
    leaves, washed

2 tablespoons chopped parsley

1 garlic clove, crushed

5 ounces ricotta cheese, drained

¾ cup soy flour

1 organic egg, plus 1 yolk

1 cup freshly grated Parmesan cheese,
    plus extra to serve

Generous grating of nutmeg

Salt and freshly ground black pepper

For the sage butter

6 tablespoons unsalted butter

Pinch of salt

16 fresh sage leaves, coarsely chopped

Serves 4

Per serving

Carbs: 6 g protein: 22 g calories: 409 fiber: 3 g fat: 33 g (saturated fat: 18 g)

Place the spinach in a bowl and add boiling water. When it has wilted, drain and let cool. Wrap a clean dish towel around the spinach and, holding it over the sink, squeeze out as much moisture as possible. Chop the spinach finely.

Combine the chopped spinach with the parsley, garlic, ricotta, soy flour, egg and egg yolk, Parmesan, and nutmeg. Season with salt and pepper. Stir vigorously until thoroughly combined.

Bring a large pan of water to a boil and salt it well. Form the dough into balls, about the size of a large cherry. (The gnocchi can be frozen at this stage if you're planning to use it for a future meal.) Drop a few gnocchi at a time into the water, lower the heat to a simmer, and cook for 3–4 minutes, or until the gnocchi have risen to the surface. Remove with a slotted spoon. Keep them warm while you cook the remaining gnocchi.

To make the sage butter, melt the butter in a pan over medium heat. Add a pinch of salt and the sage. Cook until the sage is tinged with gold. Add the herb butter to the cooked gnocchi, toss gently to coat, and serve.

Spaghetti Squash
with Smoked Chile Pesto

Some purists might say "Don't mess with pesto" but, trust me, this combination works (see also Smoky Eggplant Timbales, p.42). The noodlelike squash, with its low-key flavor, is a perfect partner for this assertive pesto. Alternatively, serve with carb-free noodles or rice, available online and from specialist suppliers.

Olive oil

1 large spaghetti squash,
    weighing about
    1 pound 10 ounces

¼ cup freshly grated Parmesan cheese
    (optional)

For the smoked chile pesto

1 dried smoked chile,
    such as chipotle (optional)

2 teaspoons smoked paprika

Large bunch of basil

⅔ cup pine nuts

2 garlic cloves, roughly chopped

½ cup freshly grated Parmesan cheese

½ teaspoon sea salt, or to taste

⅓ cup olive oil

Serves 4

Preheat the oven to 400°F. Lightly oil a baking pan. Cut the spaghetti squash in half from stem to base and scoop out the seeds and surrounding fibers. Place cut-side down on the baking pan and cook for 45–60 minutes, or until a skewer or fork pushed through the skin meets no resistance underneath. Leave until cool enough to handle. Leave the oven turned on.

Meanwhile, make the pesto. If using the dried chile, place it in a small pan with boiling water and simmer for 15–20 minutes, or until soft and rehydrated. Cool, seed, and chop. Place the remaining pesto ingredients, except the olive oil, in a food processor with the chopped chile and process until finely chopped. With the motor running, gradually add the oil until a thick paste forms.

Use a fork to pull all the spaghetti-like strands of squash away from the skin. Place in a bowl and toss with the pesto—if it seems difficult to distribute, a little splash of boiling water will help. Spoon into an ovenproof dish, scatter with the Parmesan, if using, and bake for 10–15 minutes, or until heated through. Alternatively, simply reheat in a microwave until piping hot throughout and finish with grated Parmesan.

Per serving

Carbs: 10 g protein: 13 g calories: 462 fiber: 5 g fat: 41 g (saturated fat: 8 g)

Paneer Masala
with Spinach and Coconut

I've borrowed techniques from various regions of India's vast and varied cuisine for this quick stir-fry dish. The result may not be authentic, but it is certainly an exciting combination, and amazingly simple to prepare. Use ready-made paneer or discover how easy it is to make from scratch on p.163.

2 tablespoons sunflower oil

1 teaspoon black mustard seeds

1 teaspoon cumin seeds

1 teaspoon ground turmeric

2 red chiles, slit

3 scallions, sliced

3 garlic cloves, sliced

1-inch piece of fresh ginger, chopped

heaping ½ cup desiccated coconut

11 ounces paneer, diced

2½ cups firmly packed young spinach
   leaves, washed and chopped

scant ½ cup Greek yogurt

Serves 4

Heat a wok until moderately hot. Add the oil and mustard seeds. When the seeds pop, add the cumin, turmeric, chiles, scallions, garlic, and ginger, and cook for about 2 minutes, or until golden and fragrant. Add the coconut and paneer, and cook until the paneer becomes light golden in color.

Stir the spinach through the mixture and, as soon as it is completely wilted remove the wok from the heat. Add the yogurt, stir, and serve hot.

Per serving
Carbs: 5 g protein: 12 g calories: 236 fiber: 3 g fat: 18 g (saturated fat: 10 g)

Tomato and Artichoke Stew

Canned or bottled artichoke hearts are a great convenience food and make this a sumptuous yet user-friendly dish. I originally made this dish using four large fresh artichoke hearts. Do try it with fresh if you're feeling up to the rather hairy process of removing all the leaves and the choke, then simmer them in the sauce until tender.

3 tablespoons olive oil

4 garlic cloves, crushed with
    1 teaspoon coarse salt in a mortar
    and pestle or use a garlic crusher

2 x 14-ounce cans diced tomatoes

11-ounce can or jar of artichoke
    hearts, drained and halved
    if whole

1 tablespoon red wine vinegar

2 tablespoons chopped fresh flat-leaf
    parsley, plus extra to garnish

Pinch of dried red pepper flakes

Sea salt and freshly ground
    black pepper

4 organic eggs

4–5 tablespoons ricotta cheese

Serves 4

Heat the oil in a large pan. Add the garlic and cook, stirring. As soon as it becomes fragrant, add the tomatoes and artichokes. Bring to a boil, then add the vinegar, parsley, and chile. Season to taste with salt, if necessary, and pepper. Cover and simmer gently, stirring occasionally, for 10 minutes, then remove the lid and simmer for a further 10 minutes, or until thickened.

Make four hollows with a spoon around the edge of the pan and break the eggs into them. Spoon ricotta in between the eggs. Cover the pan while the eggs cook. As soon as they are poached to your liking, serve the stew.

Per serving
Carbs: 8 g protein: 13 g calories: 233 fiber: 1.5 g fat: 17 g (saturated fat: 4 g)

Tunisian Spiced Torte

This delicious crustless mint-flavored quiche is inspired by a recipe from Tunisia called *"Makhouda nahna."* I first came across it in the book *North Africa—The Vegetarian Table* by Kitty Morse. The torte keeps for days in the refrigerator and is extremely portable, making it perfect for a picnic. Use dried mint from an herbal teabag rather than a jar or package—it tastes fresher and stronger.

Butter, for greasing

2 tablespoons olive oil

2 onions, chopped

10 organic eggs

1 cup ground almonds

Generous handful of fresh parsley, chopped

1 tablespoon dried mint

1 tablespoon mild smoked paprika/ pimentón

9 ounces Gruyère, or other aged, tangy cheese, diced

½ teaspoon salt

Freshly ground black pepper

Serves 8

Preheat the oven to 400°F. Generously grease a 9-inch springform cake pan.

Heat the olive oil over medium heat and cook the onions until lightly browned.

Beat the eggs in a large bowl, then stir in all remaining ingredients and add the onions. Stir until thoroughly combined. Pour the mixture into the prepared pan and bake for 35–40 minutes, or until a knife inserted in the middle comes out clean.

Let cool slightly, then run a sharp knife around the edge, unmold, and serve warm or at room temperature.

Per serving
Carbs: 3 g protein: 21 g calories: 345 fiber: 1 g fat: 28 g (saturated fat: 10 g)

Egg Foo Yung

I consulted Norman Fu, Chef Lecturer in Chinese Cookery, to find out the secret of this classic Anglo-Chinese dish. It requires a smart trick (outlined below) to cook it to perfection—not too leaky and not too solid. Also, the eggs are cooked over medium-low heat because, as Norman insists, "A good _foo yung_ does not have any brown bits." No spices or sauces are used, because they just mask the delicate flavors of the dish.

2½ tablespoons sunflower oil

3 tablespoons chopped red bell pepper

3 tablespoons chopped celery

3 tablespoons chopped zucchini

¼ cup beansprouts

3 scallions, sliced

4 organic eggs

Sea salt

Serves 2

Line a small colander with paper towels. Heat a well seasoned wok or nonstick skillet over high heat and add 1 teaspoon of the oil. Add the bell pepper, celery, zucchini, beansprouts, scallions, and a pinch of salt, and stir-fry for 1–2 minutes, or until softened. Transfer the contents of the pan to the lined colander and let cool and drain. This step ensures that the egg will not be diluted with cooking juices.

Beat the eggs with a little salt until combined but not frothy. Stir in the cooled vegetables and mix well. Heat the wok or pan over low to medium heat and add the remaining oil. Pour in the egg mixture and swirl it around in the pan. Push the mixture away from you while tilting the pan toward you, rather than scrambling vigorously, so the mixture runs gently onto the exposed areas of the wok. Repeat this action all over the wok until the egg is just set. Turn the whole _foo yung_ over once, then slide onto a plate and serve immediately.

Per serving
Carbs: 3.5 g protein: 16 g calories: 293 fiber: 1 g fat: 25 g (saturated fat: 5 g)

Cabbage Gratin

Here, the modest cabbage gets all dressed up in a creamy golden crust, studded with caraway, and lifted with the flavor of orange zest. Serve with steamed green beans.

1 tablespoon olive oil

3 garlic cloves, chopped

1¼-pound Savoy cabbage, trimmed weight, shredded

1¾ cups reduced-fat crème fraîche or sour cream

3 organic egg yolks

½ cup loosely packed grated cheddar cheese

Finely grated zest of 1 orange

Several fresh thyme sprigs, leaves stripped

1 teaspoon caraway seeds

Salt and freshly ground black pepper

Serves 4

Heat the oil in a pan and cook the garlic until light golden. Add the cabbage and season well. Cover and cook, stirring frequently, for about 15 minutes, or until the cabbage is tender.

Preheat the oven to 400°F. Remove the pan from the heat. If there is liquid in the pan, drain it off. Spoon the cabbage into an ovenproof dish and pack it down.

To make the custard, beat together the crème fraîche, egg yolks, cheddar cheese, orange zest, and thyme leaves with a pinch of salt. Pour the mixture onto the cabbage and scatter with the caraway seeds. Bake for 30–40 minutes, or until the top is golden and bubbling around the edges.

Per serving

Carbs: 10 g protein: 10 g calories: 323 fiber: 3.5 g fat: 26 g (saturated fat: 14 g)

Provençal Tian

The arrangement of the vegetables in three colorful stripes makes this a *pièce de résistance*, but you can just throw it all in haphazardly without affecting the flavor. The recipe makes a generous quantity—leftovers are lovely to eat cold as a salad.

Butter, for greasing

1 red bell pepper, cored and sliced into rings

¾ pound vine or plum tomatoes, sliced

¾ pound zucchini, sliced into ½-inch disks

14 ounces artichoke hearts, drained and halved

¾ pound eggplant, sliced in ¼-inch disks

¾ pound fennel, sliced

½ cup good-quality black olives

4 bay leaves

7 ounces fresh goat or feta cheese, crumbled (optional)

Freshly ground black pepper

For the dressing

¼ cup olive oil

1 tablespoon balsamic vinegar

4 garlic cloves, thinly sliced

A handful of fresh basil, shredded

2 tablespoons capers

1 teaspoon salt, or to taste

Serves 8

Preheat the oven to 400°F. Lightly butter a wide rectangular ovenproof dish. Aim to interleave each pair of vegetables with one another: place the red bell pepper and tomatoes alternately in one red stripe across the top of the dish and the zucchini and artichoke hearts in one green stripe across the bottom. Arrange the slices of eggplant and fennel down the middle.

Whisk together all the dressing ingredients and drizzle almost all of the dressing onto the vegetables as evenly as possible. Brush every exposed surface with the remaining dressing. Season with plenty of pepper and garnish with olives and bay leaves.

Roast for 45–50 minutes, or until the vegetables are soft, sizzling, and browned well around the edges. Remove from the oven and scatter the surface with crumbled goat or feta cheese, if using. Serve warm or cold.

Per serving
Carbs: 6 g protein: 9 g calories: 180 fiber: 3 g fat: 13 g (saturated fat: 6 g)

Luxury Cauliflower and Cheese

Here's my variation on the classic comfort food, best served with a very simply dressed crunchy salad.

2 large trimmed leeks, about ¾ pound

1 large cauliflower, about 1¼ pounds, broken into florets

1 teaspoon sea salt

2 bay leaves

1¼ cups water

¾ cup cream cheese

¾ cup loosely packed grated cheddar cheese

¼ cup freshly grated Parmesan cheese

½ teaspoon dried red pepper flakes, or to taste

Serves 4

Preheat the oven to 425°F. Slice the leeks quite thickly and wash well, making sure no dirt is concealed in the upper parts. Place the leeks in a large pan with a lid. Place the cauliflower florets on top. Add the salt and bay leaves and pour in the water. Cover and bring to a boil over high heat. Lower the heat and let simmer for 5 minutes.

Remove the cauliflower, leeks, and bay leaves from the pan and reserve the cooking liquid. Place the vegetables in a wide roasting pan or gratin dish in a snug single layer. Put the dish of vegetables in the oven to dry out while you prepare the cheese sauce.

Bring the reserved cooking liquid to a boil. Add the cream cheese, breaking it up with a whisk. Beat until smooth and melted. Add the grated cheese and beat until melted and thick, then remove from the heat.

Remove the vegetables from the oven and pour the cheese sauce evenly onto them. Scatter evenly with grated Parmesan and dust with dried red pepper flakes. Return to the oven and bake for about 20–30 minutes, or until golden brown and bubbly.

Per serving
Carbs: 6 g protein: 18 g calories: 422 fiber: 4 g fat: 36 g (saturated fat: 22 g)

Mashed Cauliflower and Porcini Gravy for Sausages

The vegetarian sausages available nowadays get better and better as food technology improves. Many are soy-protein based and low-carb, but do check the label. Pan-fried halloumi cheese slices also make an excellent accompaniment to the mashed cauliflower and gravy.

For the mashed cauliflower

1¼-pound cauliflower, trimmed weight
½ teaspoon salt
1 tablespoon olive oil
Generous grating of nutmeg

For the gravy

¼ ounce dried porcini mushrooms
1 cup boiling water
2 tablespoons olive oil
1 leek, chopped
Leaves stripped from 2 fresh thyme sprigs
1 bay leaf
½ cup dry vermouth or white wine
1 tablespoon cornstarch, mixed with 1 tablespoon cold water
Sea salt and freshly ground black pepper
Low-carb vegetarian sausages

Serves 4

First, make the gravy. Place the porcini mushrooms in a bowl and add the boiling water. Let soak for about 20 minutes. Fish the softened mushrooms out of the liquid, squeezing out excess moisture. Chop and set aside, reserving the soaking liquid.

Set a skillet over medium heat and add the oil. Add the chopped leek and porcini and cook for about 3 minutes, until the leek is softened. Add the herbs and vermouth or wine. Pour the reserved mushroom-soaking water through a fine strainer into the pan and season with salt and pepper. Bring to a boil. Stir in the cornstarch mixed with water and cook, stirring, until thickened. Simmer gently for a few more minutes to thicken further and to let the alcohol evaporate.

To make the mashed cauliflower, chop the cauliflower into fairly small pieces. Place in a heavy pan with the salt and oil, and stir. Cover and place over medium heat until steaming, then lower the heat to a gentle simmer. Let the cauliflower cook in its own juice for 15–20 minutes, or until very soft and collapsed. Remove the lid and let any remaining juices evaporate. Grate in a generous dose of nutmeg, then mash everything until smooth. If it still seems too wet, continue steaming over the heat, stirring frequently.

Cook the vegetarian sausages according to the manufacturer's instructions. Serve the mashed cauliflower and sausages with the porcini gravy poured on the top.

Per serving
Carbs: 10 g protein: 6 g calories: 177 fiber: 3 g fat: 10 g (saturated fat: 2 g)

Paneer and Herb Fritters

A few of these delectable, crunchy little fritters make a satisfying meal with a salad or some green vegetables. Alternatively, make tiny fritters for party nibbles. You can use ready-made paneer, or make your own using the recipe on p.163.

9 ounces paneer, grated or crumbled

½ small bunch (about 2 ounces) each fresh cilantro sprigs and mint leaves, chopped

1-inch piece of fresh ginger, finely grated

2 garlic cloves, crushed

1 teaspoon coriander seeds, crushed, or 1 teaspoon ground coriander

1 teaspoon salt

2 organic eggs

2 tablespoons soy flour

Sunflower oil, for frying

Freshly ground black pepper

Lemon wedges, to serve

1 quantity Sweet Chili Sauce (p.166), to serve

Serves 4

Add the paneer, herbs, ginger, garlic, coriander seeds, salt, eggs, and flour to a bowl, season with pepper, and mix very thoroughly to combine. Using wet hands, take walnut-sized handfuls of the mixture, then squeeze and press into little flat patties. Set aside on a plate while you make all the patties. Chill in the refrigerator until ready to cook.

Heat a shallow layer of oil in a nonstick skillet over medium heat. When hot, add the patties to the oil and cook until golden, then flip them and cook until golden all over. Drain on paper towels. Serve with lemon wedges, and Sweet Chili Sauce, if desired.

Per serving
Carbs: 4 g protein: 14 g calories: 165 fiber: 1 g fat: 10 g (saturated fat: 3 g)

Pumpkin and Egg Curry

This delicious southern-Indian-style curry can be eaten on its own as a stew or ladled over a thick bed of lightly buttered spinach (cooked from fresh or frozen). Ordinary "jack-o-lantern"-type pumpkins have the lightest carb ratio. Dense, orange-fleshed squashes, such as butternut and kabocha, will work beautifully, but they do have a slightly higher carbohydrate count.

For the spice paste

3 garlic cloves

1-inch piece of fresh ginger, grated

1 teaspoon coriander seeds

1 teaspoon cumin seeds

½ teaspoon ground turmeric

1 teaspoon dried red pepper flakes

½ teaspoon sea salt

2 tablespoons sunflower oil

½-pound pumpkin, peeled, seeded, and cut into chunks

½ pound zucchini chunks

1 cup celery slices

14-ounce can coconut milk

7-ounce can diced tomatoes

Sea salt and freshly ground black pepper

4 organic eggs

Chopped cilantro, to garnish (optional)

Serves 4

First, make the spice paste. Place all ingredients in a blender or spice grinder. Add enough water to allow the blades to run smoothly and process until to a smooth, pourable paste.

Set a wok or large skillet over medium heat. Add the oil and, when it's hot, add the pumpkin, zucchini, and celery, and stir-fry for about 2 minutes, or until starting to soften. Pour in the spice paste and stir briskly for 1–2 minutes, until fragrant and evenly distributed. Add the coconut milk and tomatoes, and season well with salt and pepper. Bring to a boil, then lower the heat to a simmer. Cook, stirring frequently, for about 30 minutes, or until the pumpkin has softened so much that it begins to melt into the thick curry sauce.

Meanwhile, cook the eggs. Place them in a small pan and cover with cold water. Bring to a boil and cook for 7 minutes, then drain and cool under cold running water. Crack and peel off the shell and slice the egg in half.

When the curry is cooked, stir well, then lay the egg halves on the surface of the curry. Simmer for 2 minutes, without stirring, until the eggs are warmed through. Scatter with cilantro leaves to serve.

Per serving

Carbs: 8 g protein: 12 g calories: 344 fiber: 1.5 g fat: 30 g (saturated fat: 3 g)

Artichokes Stuffed with Creamy Wild Mushrooms

You might call this gilding the lily because it's difficult to improve on the perfect globe artichoke, boiled whole and served with melted butter or mayonnaise. This recipe does elevate it, however, not only to red-carpet status, but renders it a complete meal with minimum effort.

2 tablespoons white wine vinegar

2 tablespoons olive oil

1 tablespoon butter

4 large fresh globe artichokes

¾ pound mixed wild mushrooms (especially morels, chanterelles and ceps), chopped into small chunks

2 teaspoons fresh thyme or lemon thyme leaves

¼ cup + 1 tablespoon dry vermouth

¾ cup mascarpone cheese

½ cup walnut halves, crushed

A handful of flat-leaf parsley leaves, chopped

Salt and freshly ground black pepper

Serves 4

Bring a large pan of water to a boil. Add the vinegar, olive oil, and plenty of salt to the water.

Meanwhile, prepare the artichokes. Cut off the stems flush with the base, and slice about one-third off the top. Pull what you can out of the middle and use a spoon to scoop out all of the hairy choke. Place in the boiling water and cook for 30–40 minutes, or until tender. They are done when a leaf pulled from near the center comes away without resistance. Drain, and use long-handled tongs to turn them upside-down in the colander until dry. Preheat the oven to 425°F.

To make the stuffing, melt the butter in a wide skillet over medium heat and add the mushrooms and thyme with a sprinkling of salt and pepper. When they have absorbed the butter and begin to soften, pour in the vermouth and cook, stirring, until it has almost all evaporated. Finally, stir in the mascarpone until the mushrooms are evenly coated.

Place the artichokes, bottom-side down, on a lined baking pan. Spoon the mixture into the middle of the drained artichokes. Scatter with crushed walnuts and bake for 10–15 minutes, or until heated through and golden on top. Garnish with chopped parsley before serving. To eat, use the leaves of the artichoke to scoop out the creamy filling.

Per serving
Carbs: 3.5 g protein: 6.5 g calories: 324 fiber: 1 g fat: 30 g (saturated fat: 14 g)

05:
NIBBLES, SNACKS, AND QUICK FIXES

It used to be so easy to reach for a sandwich or a bag of potato chips—low-carb life is different. A mouthful of impact-flavored protein or tasty, vitamin-packed vegetables are the solution, and it's still easy.

Chile-crust Brazil Nuts

Roasting brings out the best flavor in nuts, and these have an added dimension with the flavorful chile crust. When roasting nuts, it's essential to use a timer, because the short cooking time means they so easily get forgotten.

1 tablespoon olive oil

2 teaspoons dark soy sauce

1 teaspoon lemon juice

1 teaspoon sweetener

1 teaspoon paprika

½ teaspoon crushed chile flakes

1 teaspoon sesame seeds

1 cup Brazil nuts

Serves 8

Preheat the oven to 375°F. Whisk together all the ingredients except the Brazil nuts. Stir the nuts into the mixture and coat evenly. Spread them out in a single layer on a baking pan and roast, stirring every 2 minutes, until golden, about 10 minutes in total.

Cool completely, then transfer to a bowl and serve. Store in an airtight container.

Per serving
Carbs: 0.6 g protein: 2.6 g calories: 141 fiber: 0.8 g fat: 14 g (saturated fat: 3.2 g)

Olive Raisins

Virtually carbohydrate-free, olives are a great snack. This roasting technique gives them a pleasingly chewy texture. Feel free to experiment with different spices. The fennel seeds used here, for example, give a fragrant crunch.

½ pound large pitted green olives

½ teaspoon fennel seeds

½ teaspoon dried red pepper flakes

2 tablespoons olive oil

Serves 4

Preheat the oven to 400°F. Place the olives in a small ovenproof dish and stir in the remaining ingredients to coat evenly. Roast for 25–30 minutes, or until shrunken and wrinkly. Let cool before serving.

Per serving
Carbs: 0 g protein: 0.5 g calories: 100 fiber: 1.5 g fat: 11 g (saturated fat: 1.5 g)

Edam Chips

This method can be applied to some other hard cheeses, including Gouda, but in my experience, Edam gets the best results every time. A reliable nonstick pan is the only tool for the job. Presliced cheese is recommended because it may be more thinly sliced than you can manage yourself. Check the label if you are concerned about nonvegetarian rennet in the Edam.

3½ ounces Edam cheese,
    cut into 8 very thin slices

Makes 8

Arrange the cheese slices in a nonstick skillet, leaving a space of at least ½ inch between them. You may have to cook in batches if your skillet is too small. Place the skillet over the lowest possible heat.

The cheese will bubble and pop, oil will ooze out, and eventually the cheese will start to turn crisp underneath. Cook until the underside is looking dry and very slightly golden. This may take up to 15 minutes. Turn the cheese over carefully and cook the other side for about 5 minutes until crisp. Drain the cheese chips on paper towels. Serve warm or cold.

Per serving
Carbs: 0 g protein: 3 g calories: 43 fiber: 0 g fat: 3 g (saturated fat: 2 g)

Parmesan Wafers

These feather-light savory wafers are best enjoyed straight out of the oven or soon afterward. They soften slightly as they cool, but can be recrisped in the oven later (4–5 minutes at 350°F). Look for a vegetarian Parmesan substitute if you are concerned about animal rennet.

2 organic egg whites
Pinch of cream of tartar
3 tablespoons finely grated Parmesan
    cheese

Makes 8

Preheat the oven to 300°F. Beat the egg whites with the cream of tartar in a grease-free bowl until stiff but not dry. Gently fold in the Parmesan, keeping the mixture light and airy, until evenly incorporated. Spoon onto a baking sheet lined with wax or parchment paper to make 8 wafers. Bake for about 15 minutes, or until golden and crisp.

Per serving
Carbs: 0 g protein: 1.5 g calories: 13 fiber: 0 g fat: 0.7 g (saturated fat: 0.5 g)

Mexican Cucumbers

I was first introduced to these in Mexico, where they are served as bar snacks—it's a surprisingly good combination. The mild chile powder I use is a commonly sold mixture with added garlic powder and oregano. A ready-made "taco seasoning" also works well.

1 medium-sized cucumber,
   about 11 ounces in weight
Juice of 2 limes
2 teaspoons mild chile powder mix
   or taco seasoning mix
Sea salt

Serves 8

Trim the ends of the cucumber, then cut it across into four pieces of equal length. Cut each piece lengthwise into eight wedges. Arrange the wedges skin-side down in a dish and squeeze the juice from the limes over them. Dust with an even coat of mild chile powder and season with salt.

Per serving
Carbs: 0.5 g protein: 0.3 g calories: 4 fiber: 0.3 g fat: 0 g (saturated fat: 0 g)

Spicy Tofu Biltong

Deeply flavored and toothsome, these do a surprisingly good job of imitating beef jerky or biltong.

7 ounces smoked or plain tofu
(flavored or premarinated
can also be used)
2 tablespoons dark soy sauce
2 tablespoons dry sherry
1 teaspoon rice vinegar
Pinch of cayenne pepper
1 tablespoon sunflower oil

Makes 14

Preheat the oven to 250°F. Pat the tofu dry with paper towels, then slice very thinly into about 14 strips, 1 inch wide, 3 inches long, and roughly ⅛ inch thick.

Line a baking pan with nonstick parchment paper. Thoroughly beat all the remaining ingredients together in a shallow dish. Dip each piece of tofu in the mixture, then arrange them on the baking pan. Spoon any remaining mixture carefully all over the tofu strips.

Place in the oven and cook for about 60–80 minutes, or until the tofu is crisp around the edges, but still pliable. Let cool. The strips can be stored in an airtight container in the refrigerator for up to 3 days.

Per serving
Carbs: 0.3 g protein: 1 g calories: 21 fiber: 0 g fat: 1.5 g (saturated fat: 0.2 g)

Sesame and Black Pepper Crispbreads

When you really miss that cracker-crunch, these are a godsend. Cooking this batter in a microwave seems to be the only way to get a super-crisp result. They are a great companion to the soups in this book.

2 tablespoons sesame seeds

Olive oil, for brushing

½ cup soy flour

1 organic egg

½ teaspoon salt

½ cup warm water

1 teaspoon freshly ground black pepper

Makes 8

First toast the sesame seeds. Heat a dry skillet over medium heat. Add the sesame seeds and toast, stirring frequently, until golden and popping. Remove from the pan and set aside.

Line a microwave-safe plate with nonstick parchment paper. Brush it generously with olive oil. Beat together the flour, egg, salt, water, and pepper until smooth. Pour a thin layer of batter onto the plate, about 2½ inches in diameter. Scatter with sesame seeds. Microwave on high for 1½–3 minutes, until dry and crisp. Cooking time will depend on the microwave. Transfer to a wire rack to cool. Repeat with the remaining batter. Store in an airtight container.

Per serving
Carbs: 1.5 g protein: 4 g calories: 65 fiber: 1 g fat: 5 g (saturated fat: 0.8 g)

Marinated Crudité Salad

Here's a fantastic way of preparing raw vegetables. These will keep in the refrigerator for a few days, ready to munch on any occasion.

½ red bell pepper, cored
½ yellow bell pepper, cored
3½ ounces sugar snap peas
3½ ounces fine green beans, trimmed
2 ounces zucchini
2 ounces celery
3½ ounces fennel
1 tablespoon sea salt
1 tablespoon lemon juice
1 tablespoon extra-virgin olive oil

Serves 4

If the vegetable lends itself to being cut into strips, do so; others can be cut into similar-sized pieces (for example, beans and fennel).

Place them all in a bowl and scatter with the salt. Toss with your hands to coat evenly. Transfer to a colander and place over a bowl that will fit in the fridge. Cover with plastic wrap and refrigerate, stirring occasionally, for 3–4 hours.

Shake the vegetables in the colander to drain thoroughly (do not rinse). Place the vegetables in a clean bowl, add lemon juice and olive oil, and stir. Store covered in the fridge, ideally in a plastic container with a secure lid so you can shake it occasionally to bring the flavorful juices back up to dress the vegetables.

Per serving
Carbs: 5 g protein: 2 g calories: 57 fiber: 2.5 g fat: 3 g (saturated fat: 0.5 g)

Celery with Pesto

Here's an easy solution when you're in the mood to raid the refrigerator. You can use ready-made pesto or make your own (see p.165).

2 celery sticks, trimmed

2 tablespoons cream cheese

1–2 teaspoons pesto

Freshly ground black pepper

Serves 2

Use a butter knife to spread the cream cheese inside the curve of the celery. Drizzle pesto down the middle. Grind some pepper onto it, then eat whole or slice diagonally into bite-sized pieces.

Per serving
Carbs: 0.4 g protein: 0.6 g calories: 70 fiber: 0.3 g fat: 7 g (saturated fat: 4 g)

06:
PARTY
FOOD

Canapés and finger food should be easy to make, easy to eat, beautiful, luxurious, and hard to resist. It's all possible with the recipes in this chapter. Enjoy with champagne or vodka martinis.

Eggplant and Smoked Cheese Involtini

Involtini simply means "little rolls" in Italian. In this case, chargrilled eggplant slices encase little rod-shaped pieces of melting smoked cheese, which ideally should be a smoked mozzarella, but it's rather a privilege to come across the real thing, so any smoked cheese will do. Pictured here with Green Bean and Roasted Bell Pepper Parcels (see p.116).

2 eggplants, about 1¼ pounds, stem removed and sliced lengthwise as thinly as possible

¼ cup olive oil

25 large basil leaves

3½ ounces smoked mozzarella, smoked cheddar, or other smoked cheese, cut in 25 pieces, measuring about ¾ x ¼ inch

Sea salt and freshly ground black pepper

Makes 25

Heat a ridged grill pan for about 10 minutes, or until very hot. Brush the eggplant slices lightly on both sides with olive oil. Cook on the grill pan until soft and striped with black on both sides. Season each slice with salt and pepper and let cool.

Place a basil leaf at one end of an eggplant slice and a piece of cheese on top of the basil. Roll the slice up around the cheese and basil. Place, seam-side down, on a cookie sheet. Repeat with the remaining ingredients.

Preheat the oven to 400°F. Just before serving, put the involtini in the oven for no longer than 5 minutes just to warm through—it's best to set a timer or they might overcook if forgotten. Serve warm and melting.

Per serving
Carbs: 0.5 g protein: 1 g calories: 30 fiber: 0.5 g fat: 3 g (saturated fat: 1 g)

Green Bean and Roasted Bell Pepper Parcels

Simplicity itself, beautiful to behold, and even more gorgeous to eat. Don't save these just for a party—you should spoil yourself and your family with them, too, as a neat little appetizer or accompaniment. Freshly made roasted peppers always tastes best, but if you're really pushed for time, use roasted peppers from a jar or can, or buy them from the deli counter. Pictured on p.115.

2 red bell peppers

3½ ounces fine green beans, trimmed

¼ cup cream cheese

8 fresh basil leaves, shredded

Sea salt and freshly ground black
    pepper

Makes 8

Preheat the broiler to its highest setting. Cut the bell peppers in half from stem to base and remove the cores and stems. Place, cut-side down, on a baking sheet lined with nonstick parchment paper. Broil the bell peppers until blackened and blistered all over. Transfer to a plastic bag. Seal and let cool.

Meanwhile, bring a small pan of water to a boil and add salt. Cook the green beans for 2–3 minutes, or until just tender but still bright green. Drain and cool under cold running water. Pat dry.

Peel the skins carefully off of the peppers, being careful not to tear the flesh. Cut each half in half again from stem end to base. Set the halves on a cutting board, peeled-side down. Place about a rounded teaspoonful of cream cheese on the surface of each piece, then scatter with basil. Grind a little salt and pepper onto them. Lay a bundle of 4–5 green beans across the top and wrap the pepper around the beans. Place seam-side down on a plate and chill in the refrigerator until ready to serve.

Per serving
Carbs: 3 g protein: 1 g calories: 48 fiber: 1 g fat: 4 g (saturated fat: 2 g)

Tricolore Skewers

The three colors of the Italian flag, in one bite, on a skewer. Use buffalo mozzarella for the creamiest flavor; failing that, use cow mozarella, but always from a snow-white ball, not the "pizza cheese" type.

1 buffalo mozzarella,
    torn into 24 bite-sized shreds
24 semidried or sundried tomatoes
    in oil
24 large fresh basil leaves

Makes 24

Pair up a piece of mozzarella and a tomato. Wrap a basil leaf around them and secure with a medium-length bamboo skewer. Serve immediately.

Per serving

Carbs: 0.1 g protein: 1.5 g calories: 29 fiber: 0 g fat: 2.5 g (saturated fat: 1 g)

Cucumber
with Pink Pickled Ginger

Pink pickled ginger is an essential accompaniment for sushi and can be found in Asian supermarkets and health-food stores. Look for the shredded psychedelic-fuchsia type (you can't miss it!), for maximum visual impact, or use the traditional light-pink type.

1 quantity Satay Sauce (see p.169)
Half a cucumber (about 5 inches long,
    weighing about 7 ounces)
¼ cup pink pickled ginger
1 scallion,
    finely sliced diagonally

Makes 20

Cool the Satay Sauce, then chill until thick.

Peel the cucumber and cut into 20 slices, ¼ inch thick. (If desired, you can make neat shapes with a small cookie cutter.)

Spoon a small dollop of Satay Sauce on each piece, then place a pinch of pickled ginger on top. Garnish with a slice of scallion.

Per serving

Carbs: 0.6 g protein: 0.6 g calories: 16 fiber: 0.2 g fat: 1 g (saturated fat: 0.3 g)

Cucumber and Tofu Satay

On a day-to-day basis, I wouldn't normally play around threading morsels onto skewers for supper, which is why this recipe lands in the Party Food chapter. However, I think you'll find these are easy and tasty enough to enjoy without a special occasion. Freezing the tofu gives it a remarkable fibrous texture that resembles chicken, so try the technique given below in other tofu dishes, too. Or simply use fresh firm tofu.

3½ ounces firm tofu

3½ ounces cucumber

1 quantity Satay Sauce
    (see p.169)

1 quantity Sweet Chili Sauce
    (see p.166) (optional)

Makes 12

Freeze the tofu until absolutely solid, then thaw completely before using. Drain thoroughly and wrap in paper towels. Place on a plate and weigh down with a heavy object, such as a pan of water—this will compress the tofu slightly and squeeze out excess moisture. Leave for about 30 minutes, then cut into small cubes about ½ inch wide.

Cut the cucumber into strips the same width and remove the seeds. Cut into pieces the same size as the tofu. Thread alternating pieces of tofu and cucumber onto 12 medium-length bamboo skewers, using three of each per skewer. Arrange the skewers side by side on a plate. Spoon Satay Sauce generously all over them and serve, adding Sweet Chili Sauce if desired.

Per serving
Carbs: 1 g protein: 2 g calories: 32 fiber: 0.5 g fat: 2.5 g (saturated fat: 0.5 g)

Saffron Aïoli
with Quail Eggs and Asparagus

Quail eggs are wonderfully elegant, but undeniably awkward to peel. They are so beautiful in the shell that I always leave it on and let the guests do the work.

24 quail eggs

3 bunches asparagus,
    woody ends snapped off

5 garlic cloves (or to taste), central
    sprouts removed, if any

3 organic egg yolks

½ teaspoon saffron threads, soaked in
    1 tablespoon hot water

Salt

1 cup light olive oil

2 tablespoons lemon juice

Serves 8

Place the quail eggs in a pan and cover with cold water. Bring to a boil and cook for 3 minutes. Drain and cool under cold running water until completely cold.

Steam the asparagus until barely tender, or cooked to your liking. Let cool.

Put the garlic in a food processor and process until finely chopped. Place the egg yolks, soaked saffron with its soaking water, and a little salt in a food processor and process to combine. With the motor running, add the oil, one drop at a time. Gradually increase the pace and pour in the remaining oil in a very thin, steady stream until a thick mayonnaise is achieved. If the aïoli curdles, add another egg yolk.

Beat in the lemon juice. Scoop into a bowl and serve on a platter with quail eggs and asparagus.

Per serving
Carbs: 1.5 g protein: 13 g calories: 365 fiber: 1.3 g fat: 34 g (saturated fat: 6 g)

Chile Citrus Labneh Platter

Labneh is a soft fresh cheese from the Middle East made by transforming yogurt overnight in the refrigerator. It couldn't be simpler and you can flavor it with whatever you like—fresh or dried herbs, or whole toasted spices, such as cumin. This red chile and citrus version is particularly pretty and the flavor just dances on the tongue. Be sure you remove only the outer zest of the orange and lemon and none of the bitter white pith.

2 cups Greek yogurt or other full-fat
  yogurt
2 hot red chiles, chopped
grated zest of 1 orange
grated zest of 1 lemon
extra-virgin olive oil,
  for drizzling
Salt

To serve
About 1¼ pounds raw vegetables,
  such as celery sticks, bell pepper
  strips, cucumber batons, sugar
  snap peas

Serves 8

Line a small, fine strainer with a piece of muslin or cheesecloth. The shape of your strainer will determine the shape of the labneh—a conical shape is attractive. Set the strainer over a deep bowl (make sure there is space for it in your refrigerator) so there is plenty of room for the whey to drain into the bowl.

Mix the yogurt thoroughly with the chiles, citrus zests, and a generous pinch of salt for maximum flavor. Scoop the mixture into the lined strainer and it smooth down. Cover with plastic wrap and place in the refrigerator for 24–36 hours. Invert the labneh and lining onto a plate, removed the lining, and drizzle the labneh with olive oil. Arrange the vegetables around the labneh and serve, using a butter knife to spread it with.

Per serving
Carbs: 3 g protein: 3 g calories: 58 fiber: 0 g fat: 4 g (saturated fat: 2.5 g)

Hot Artichoke Sin

I call this "Sin" as a reminder that it is pure indulgence, and that's also why it resides in the Party Food chapter. It does not look particularly elegant, but the taste never fails to please.

14-ounce can artichoke hearts, drained and chopped
½ cup mayonnaise
½ cup freshly grated Parmesan cheese
2 large green chiles, seeded and chopped
1 organic egg

Serves 8

Preheat the oven to 425°F. Mix together the artichoke hearts, mayonnaise, cheese, and chiles in a bowl. Beat in the egg. Spread the mixture into a wide ovenproof dish in a layer no more than ¾ inch deep.

Bake for about 30 minutes, or until bubbling and very dark golden on top and bottom. Remove from the oven and let cool.

To serve, slide onto a cutting board and cut into bite-sized squares with a knife or pizza wheel.

Per serving
Carbs: 5 g protein: 5 g calories: 176 fiber: 2 g fat: 15 g (saturated fat: 3.5 g)

Smoked Eggplant Purée

This dip is also known as *Baba Ganoush*. Cooking the eggplant directly over a naked flame gives it a mystical smoky flavor, while softening it to a pulp. If you don't cook using gas, see instructions on how to do this in the oven, below.

2 medium-sized eggplants

1 garlic clove

2 tablespoons lemon juice

2 tablespoons extra-virgin olive oil

3 tablespoons Greek yogurt

Coarse salt and freshly ground
    black pepper

To serve

About 1¼ pounds raw vegetables,
    such as celery sticks, bell pepper
    strips, cucumber batons, Little
    Gem lettuce leaves, Belgian endive
    leaves

Serves 8

Push a fork into the stem of an eggplant and hold directly in a high gas flame. Turn occasionally until completely soft and collapsed; the skin should be blackened to the point of ash in places, and steam should be escaping through the fork holes. Repeat with the second eggplant. Alternatively, preheat the oven to its highest setting. Prick the eggplants a few times, place on a cookie sheet and roast until completely soft.

Transfer to a plate and leave to cool. Peel off the charred skins. Don't worry if a few little charred flecks remain because they will add to the flavor. Place the flesh in a bowl.

Crush the garlic clove with a little coarse salt in a mortar and pestle for the best flavor. Alternatively, use a garlic crusher. Using a fork, break up the eggplants, then mash together with the crushed garlic and remaining ingredients, until fairly smooth. Season to taste.

Per serving
Carbs: 2 g protein: 1 g calories: 41 fiber: 1.5 g fat: 3.5 g (saturated fat: 0.7 g)

07:
ON THE SIDE

The best vegetarian meal is a balanced composition of flavors and textures on a plate. None of these recipes need play second fiddle, but become part of a richly varied menu when paired up with other dishes.

Avocado and Lemon Salad

Small pieces of whole lemon and a ginger-spiked dressing complement the creamy, rich avocado. Serve this with Red Bell Pepper and Goat Cheese Timbales (see p.45).

1 lemon

2 ripe avocados

Sea salt, to taste

1 teaspoon finely grated fresh ginger

¼ cup extra-virgin olive oil

4 handfuls young spinach leaves
(about 3½ ounces)

Serves 4

Halve the lemon. Squeeze and strain the juice from one half into a small pitcher for the dressing. Cut the other half in half again and then slice as thinly as possible.

Peel, halve, and seed the avocados. Cut the flesh into quarters, then slice.

Mix the salt and ginger into the lemon juice, then gradually whisk in the olive oil.

Arrange the spinach leaves on a platter or individual plates. Place the avocado and lemon slices on top. Drizzle with the dressing and serve immediately.

Per serving
Carbs: 2 g protein: 2.5 g calories: 247 fiber: 3 g fat: 25 g (saturated fat: 4 g)

Ruby Chard
with Pine Nuts and Red Currants

Tart, blushing red currants are sublime with the earthy chard. A handful of cranberries could be substituted off-season—add them to the pan with the pine nuts. Serve this with Eggplant Rarebit (see p.50) or Creamy Celeriac Gratin (see p.76).

1 pound ruby chard with stalks, or
　　beet greens or Swiss chard
2 tablespoons olive oil
2 tablespoons pine nuts
⅓ cup red currants
Salt and freshly ground black pepper

Serves 2–4

Wash and dry the chard or greens, strip the leaves, and chop them coarsely. Chop the stalks into ¾-inch wide pieces.

Heat the oil in a pan and add the pine nuts. Cook, stirring, until the nuts are golden. Add the chard stalks, season with salt and pepper, and stir. Cover the pan and cook, stirring occasionally, for about 3 minutes, until softened. Add chopped leaves, cover, and cook until just wilted.

Transfer the mixture to a platter using a slotted spoon and scatter with the red currants.

Per serving
Carbs: 4 g protein: 3 g calories: 119 fiber: 0.5 g fat: 10 g (saturated fat: 1 g)

Braised Fennel and Bell Peppers

This bold and rustic Mediterranean side dish is the ideal foil for Arugula and Ricotta Cheesecake (see p.72), Roasted Eggplant with Dill Sauce (see p.133), or an omelet.

3 tablespoons olive oil

2 fennel bulbs, trimmed and sliced

1 red bell pepper, cored and sliced

1 yellow bell pepper, cored and sliced

3–4 fresh thyme sprigs

1 teaspoon coriander seeds

1 teaspoon dried red pepper flakes

10 extra-large green olives

2 garlic cloves, crushed

½ cup red wine

Salt and freshly ground black pepper

Serves 4

Heat the oil in a wide skillet over medium heat and add the fennel, peppers, and thyme. Cook, stirring frequently, until the vegetables are beginning to soften and brown.

Add the coriander seeds, dried red pepper flakes, and olives, season with salt and pepper, and cook for a further 5 minutes. Add the garlic and cook very briefly until fragrant, then add the wine. Simmer until the liquid has evaporated.

Per serving

Carbs: 6 g protein: 1 g calories: 136 fiber: 3 g fat: 10 g (saturated fat: 1.5 g)

Roasted Eggplant with Dill Sauce

Here, the hot eggplants are doused in a cool, creamy sauce to create a warm salad—very nice in its own right, with crunchy lettuce leaves. Also try it with Halloumi-stuffed Bell Peppers (see p.48) or Braised Fennel and Bell Peppers (see p.132).

2 large eggplants

Olive oil, for brushing

1 cup Greek yogurt

3 tablespoons chopped fresh dill,
   or 2 tablespoons freeze-dried dill

Grated zest of 1 lemon

Juice of ½ lemon

1 small garlic clove, crushed

Salt and freshly ground black pepper

Serves 4

Preheat the oven to 425°F. Chop the stems off the eggplants and cut the eggplants into six long wedges from top to bottom. Score the flesh diagonally without piercing the skin. Brush generously with olive oil and place, flesh-side down, in a roasting pan. Season with salt and pepper. Roast for about 30 minutes, or until soft and tinged with gold.

Meanwhile, make the sauce. Combine all the remaining ingredients thoroughly. Spoon the sauce onto the hot eggplant and serve.

Per serving
Carbs: 4 g protein: 4 g calories: 115 fiber: 1 g fat: 9 g (saturated fat: 5 g)

Turnip Dauphinoise

I scanned dozens of French cookbooks searching for the ultimate Potato Dauphinoise recipe, but in the end I took a cue from stylish London cook, Alastair Hendy, who makes a warm cream infusion and adds chives to his. Believe me, low-carb turnips plug into this classic dish as if they were always meant to be there. To make life easy, use a food processor with a slicing blade for the turnips if you can. Celeriac can be substituted for turnips, without gaining any carbs.

1 tablespoon butter, for greasing

2¼ pounds turnips, trimmed weight, peeled and thinly sliced

Sea salt and freshly ground black pepper

1 large bunch of chives, chopped

1 garlic clove, halved

1 cup heavy cream

1 cup sour cream

scant ½ cup water

Serves 6

Preheat the oven to 325°F. Butter a medium-sized gratin dish.

Make layers of turnip slices, seasoning them with salt and pepper and scattering them with chopped chives as you go.

Place the garlic, cream, sour cream, and water in a pan. Gradually bring to just below boiling point, stirring constantly, then remove from the heat. Pour the mixture onto the turnips but remove and discard the garlic halves.

Bake for 1¼–1½ hours, or until the turnips are fork-tender throughout.

Per serving

Carbs: 10 g protein: 3 g calories: 349 fiber: 4 g fat: 33 g (saturated fat: 20 g)

Mashed Pumpkin and Turnips

This velvety purée is the ideal accompaniment to any particularly juicy dish. Try it with Portobello Mushrooms with Blue Cheese Custard (see p.46) or, if you're feeding a crowd, Provençal Tian (see p.89). This dish freezes well for future convenience.

1¼-pound pumpkin, trimmed weight, seeded, peeled, and cubed

1¼-pound turnip, trimmed weight, peeled and cubed

1 cup water

2 tablespoons whipping cream

Whole nutmeg, for grating

Sea salt and freshly ground black pepper

Serves 6

Place the pumpkin and turnip in a pan and add water to cover and a pinch of salt. Cover, bring to a boil, and cook for 20–30 minutes, or until very tender and collapsing. Drain thoroughly (the cooking liquid is a delicious stock which you could save or freeze).

Return the vegetables to the pan and place over low heat to steam off excess moisture for 5 minutes, stirring frequently. Remove the pan from the heat, add the cream, and a very generous grating of nutmeg. Mash to a smooth purée. Season to taste with salt and pepper and serve.

Per serving
Carbs: 6 g protein: 1 g calories: 50 fiber: 2.5 g fat: 2.5 g (saturated fat: 1 g)

Greens in Coconut Milk

Even those who need a little persuasion to eat their greens might find these hard to refuse. Use Savoy cabbage, kale, collard greens, or chard. Brussels sprout tops and rapini (broccoli rabe) also like this treatment.

1 tablespoon olive oil

11 ounces greens, trimmed weight, coarsely chopped or torn

1-inch piece of fresh ginger, minced

14 fluid ounce can coconut milk

1 teaspoon ground cumin

Sea salt and freshly ground black pepper

Serves 4

Place a large pan over medium heat and add the oil. Add the greens and ginger, cover, and cook, stirring occasionally, for about 2 minutes, or until bright green and wilted.

Add the coconut milk and cumin, season with salt and pepper, and cook, uncovered, for 5 minutes, or until the greens are cooked to your liking. Serve hot.

Per serving

Carbs: 5 g protein: 5 g calories: 222 fiber: 1.5 g fat: 20 g (saturated fat: 12 g)

Baby Zucchini with Mint and Vinegar

When you see baby zucchini on sale, grab them. They are succulent and naturally sweet. If they have flowers attached, so much the better because this means that they are really fresh and you can add the flowers to this recipe, too. Bulk this up into a main course by adding some slices of buffalo mozzarella and a few arugula leaves. The zucchini can also be cooked on a ridged grill pan. Toss them with the oil in a bowl first, then cook on a preheated grill pan.

1 pound 5 ounces baby zucchini

2 tablespoons olive oil

1½ tablespoons white wine vinegar

A handful of fresh mint leaves, coarsely chopped

Salt and freshly ground black pepper

Serves 4

If the zucchini really are young, there's no need to trim them, unless there is a withered flower on one end. If they are larger, trim both ends. Slice in half lengthwise.

Add the oil to a large, nonstick skillet over low heat and gently cook the zucchini until well-colored on each side, then transfer to a plate. You may have to do this in batches. As each batch comes out of the pan, sprinkle with a little vinegar and season with salt and pepper while still warm. Let the zucchini cool completely.

Scatter with the chopped mint and finish with extra pepper to serve.

Per serving
Carbs: 2.5 g protein: 2.6 g calories: 76 fiber: 1.5 g fat: 6 g (saturated fat: 1 g)

08:
SWEET THINGS

Got a sweet tooth? Satisfy it here. With these gratifying sugar-free treats you don't have to deny yourself an indulgent dessert from time to time.

Berry Gratin

To enjoy this at its absolute best, a powerful broiler is the key, so that the berries are quickly heated to the point of nearly bursting—then they collapse on the tongue.

14 ounces mixed berries,
    especially blackberries,
    raspberries, and blueberries
¼ cup sweetener
⅔ cup cream cheese
generous ¼ cup whipping cream
Juice of ½ a lemon
Coarsely grated zest of 1 lemon

Serves 6

Preheat the broiler to its highest setting. Place the berries in a gratin dish, add 1 tablespoon of the sweetener, and toss to coat the berries.

Beat together the cream cheese, whipping cream, the remaining sweetener, and the lemon juice in a bowl. Spoon the mixture onto the berries in an even layer, covering most of the surface but leaving a border of berries around the edge. Scatter with the lemon zest.

Broil for about 5 minutes, or until the topping is patched with gold and the berries are swollen. Serve immediately.

Per serving
Carbs: 4 g protein: 2 g calories: 174 fiber: 2 g fat: 17 g (saturated fat: 10 g)

Chocolate Marzipan Cheesecake

A very indulgent cheesecake—with a knockout chocolate flavor and silky texture—perched on a marzipan crust.

For the crust

1 cup ground almonds

3½ tablespoons butter, melted

2 tablespoons sweetener

½ teaspoon almond extract

Good pinch of salt

For the topping

1½ cups cream cheese

¾ cup mascarpone cheese

6 tablespoons sweetener

2 organic eggs

5 ounces dark diabetic chocolate,
   melted

Fresh raspberries, shaved diabetic
   chocolate, and cocoa powder,
   to garnish (optional)

Serves 10

Preheat the oven to 300°F. Add all the ingredients for the crust to a bowl and stir to form a thick paste. Press firmly and evenly into the bottom of an 8-inch cake pan with a removable bottom. Leave in the frige to chill while you prepare the topping.

Beat together the two cheeses in a bowl with an electric blender or process in a food processor. Beat in the sweetener and eggs and finally the chocolate, beating until smooth. Pour the batter into the chilled crust and bake for 30–40 minutes, or until set but still slightly wobbly in the middle.

Let cool in the pan (it will set further as it cools). When completely cold, chill in the refrigerator for 3 hours or overnight before serving.

Carbs: 6 g protein: 7 g calories: 402 fiber: 1 g fat: 39 g (saturated fat: 21 g)

Coconut Ice Cream

This has to be the simplest ice cream ever. Remember to remove it from the freezer at least 30 minutes before serving, or longer. When stirred, you get a floppy, whipped texture just like soft ice cream from an ice cream stand. Try it with a spoonful of Raspberry Purée (see p.165) drizzled over it.

14 fluid ounce can coconut milk

scant cup heavy cream

⅓ cup sweetener

Serves 8

Beat all the ingredients together until thoroughly combined. Chill in the refrigerator, then place in an ice-cream maker and follow the manufacturer's instructions.

To freeze the ice cream manually, pour the chilled mixture into a large, shallow plastic container with an airtight lid. Cover and place in the coldest part of the freezer for 1–1½ hours. Remove the container from the freezer and stir the mixture vigorously or beat with an electric mixer, incorporating the ice crystals that will have formed around the edge into the rest of the slush. Cover the container again and return it to the freezer. Repeat this twice more every 2 hours, or until the ice cream is thick throughout. Freeze until ready to serve, but let stand at room temperature for at least 30 minutes and stir just before serving.

Per serving
Carbs: 2.5 g protein: 2 g calories: 214 fiber: 0 g fat: 22 g (saturated fat: 15 g)

Coffee Ice Cream

This is a traditional custard-based ice cream. Once you taste the coffee-flavored custard, you may decide not to freeze it at all and simply devour it as a dessert—it's virtually irresistible.

1¼ cups whipping cream

3 organic egg yolks

3 tablespoons sweetener

1 tablespoon instant coffee powder

Serves 4

Pour the cream into a pan and gradually bring to just below boiling point over low to medium heat.

Meanwhile, whisk together the egg yolks, sweetener, and instant coffee powder in a pitcher. The coffee may not immediately dissolve, but don't worry, it soon will.

When the cream just starts to bubble around the edges, remove from the heat and gradually pour it into the egg mixture, beating constantly. Pour the mixture back into the pan and place it over low heat. Continue beating until the mixture becomes thick and coats the back of a wooden spoon.

Pour the mixture back into the rinsed-out pitcher. Cover with plastic wrap and pierce the top so that the steam can escape. Let cool, then chill in the refrigerator.

Pour into an ice-cream maker and follow the manufacturer's instructions. Alternatively, follow the instructions for manual ice-cream making, as for Coconut Ice Cream (see p.146).

Per serving
Carbs: 2 g protein: 4 g calories: 331 fiber: 0 g fat: 34 g (saturated fat: 20 g)

Lemon Custard Macaroon Tart

Dried coconut makes a perfectly golden, sweet, and crispy crust.

1¾ cups desiccated coconut

3 organic eggs: 2 separated,
    plus 1 yolk

7 tablespoons sweetener

Butter, for greasing

½ cup heavy cream

Finely grated zest of 2 lemons

Juice of 1 lemon

Raspberries, to garnish (optional)

Serves 8

Preheat oven to 350°F. Combine the coconut, 2 egg whites, and 3 tablespoons of the sweetener in a bowl. Blend until well mixed and sticky. Generously grease an 8-inch nonstick fluted French tart pan with a removable bottom. Or, use 8 small individual tartlet pans. Press the coconut mixture firmly into the bottom and up the sides. Place on a cookie sheet and bake for 5 minutes.

To make the filling, beat together the 3 egg yolks, the remaining sweetener, the cream, and the lemon zest and juice. Remove the tart crust from the oven and pour in the filling. Return to the oven for 15 minutes, until patched with gold. (If you are using individual tartlet pans keep an eye on them because the cooking time will be reduced.)

Let cool completely before removing from the pan, using the end of a small knife to loosen the edges.

Per serving (ungarnished)
Carbs: 2 g protein: 2 g calories: 226 fiber: 3 g fat: 24 g (saturated fat: 17 g)

Zabaglione

There's a fair amount of continuous whisking involved in making zabaglione, so it's most comfortably made for just two people. It should also be eaten immediately—warm, boozy, and frothy. It's a wonderful spontaneous dessert. Enjoy on its own or with 1–2 spoonfuls of Raspberry Purée (see p.165) stirred through.

4 organic egg yolks

2 tablespoons sweetener

¼ cup Marsala wine
    or Madeira or sherry

Serves 2

Pour about a 1-inch depth of water into a pan, over which you can set a small heatproof glass bowl. Bring to a boil.

Meanwhile, beat all the ingredients together in the heatproof bowl until evenly combined. Reduce the boiling water to a simmer and set the bowl over it. Whisk constantly for 4–5 minutes, until the mixture has nearly tripled in volume and begins to hold its shape. Serve immediately.

Per serving

Carbs: 4 g protein: 37 g calories: 450 fiber: 0 g fat: 27 g (saturated fat: 8 g)

Cardamom Cake

Cardamom has the ability to make things taste sweeter, so I knew it would be ideal in a low-carb recipe. A sliver of this light sponge cake is perfect with coffee or afternoon tea.

Butter, for greasing

¾ cup soy flour

½ cup ground almonds

1 teaspoon baking powder

1 teaspoon cardamom seeds,
    out of the pod, crushed

5 tablespoons sweetener

2 organic eggs

3 tablespoons reduced-fat crème
    fraîche or sour cream

3 tablespoons sunflower oil

1 tablespoon vanilla extract

Generous pinch of salt

Serves 8

Preheat the oven to 350°F. Grease the inside of an 8-inch cake pan and line the bottom with parchment paper.

Stir together the flour, ground almonds, baking powder, and cardamom seeds in a small bowl.

In a separate bowl, beat together the sweetener, eggs, crème fraîche or sour cream, oil, vanilla, and salt using an electric mixer or by hand. Stir the dry ingredients into the wet, combining thoroughly, but do not overwork. Pour into the prepared pan and bake for 20 minutes, or until golden and set. Let rest for 5 minutes in the pan, then remove from the pan and transfer to a wire rack to finish cooling.

Per serving
Carbs: 3 g protein: 7.5 g calories: 140 fiber: 5 g fat: 11 g (saturated fat: 1.8 g)

Cream Cheese
and Macadamia Nut Brownies

High-impact, real brownies, studded with rich macadamia nuts and pockets of baked cream cheese.

5 ounces dark diabetic chocolate, chopped

7 tablespoons butter

3 organic eggs

5 tablespoons sweetener

1 teaspoon vanilla extract

¾ cup soy flour

1 teaspoon baking powder

Pinch of salt

¾ cup coarsely chopped unsalted macadamia nuts

heaping ¼ cup chilled cream cheese, cut into small cubes

Makes 12

Preheat the oven to 350°F. Line a small rectangular cake pan or ovenproof dish with parchment paper.

Melt the chocolate and butter together in a heatproof bowl set over a pan of simmering water. Alternatively, melt in the microwave. Stir until smooth, then let cool slightly.

Beat together the eggs, sweetener, and vanilla in a large bowl. Add the chocolate mixture and combine thoroughly. Sift the flour, baking powder, and salt onto the mixture, add the nuts, and stir until just combined.

Pour the batter into the prepared pan or dish and smooth the surface. Dot with the cream cheese. Bake for 30–40 minutes, or until firm. Cool, then cut into 12 squares.

Per serving
Carbs: 7 g protein: 6 g calories: 257 fiber: 1 g fat: 23 g (saturated fat: 10 g)

Rose and Raspberry Pudding

The delicate flavor of rose water is the surprise element in this raspberry-flecked custard. I like to use frozen raspberries because they ooze their magenta juices as they defrost in the cooling pudding. Rose water varies greatly in strength, so start with a smaller amount and increase if desired.

1 cup fresh or frozen raspberries

6 organic egg yolks

¼ cup sweetener

1–3 tablespoons rose water, to taste

2½ cups heavy cream

1 vanilla bean

Serves 6

Divide the raspberries among 6 individual wine glasses or small glass dessert dishes and set aside.

Place the egg yolks, sweetener, and rose water in a large bowl and beat by hand with a wire whisk until smooth.

Pour the cream into a pan. Slit the vanilla bean lengthwise and scrape out the seeds into the cream, then add the bean to the cream as well and bring gently to just below simmering point—it should just start to bubble around the edges. Remove the bean and gradually pour the hot cream onto the egg mixture, whisking constantly. Pour the mixture back into the pan and whisk over low heat until thick. Pour the custard into the prepared glasses or bowls. Let cool, then chill before serving.

Per serving
Carbs: 3 g protein: 5 g calories: 563 fiber: 0.6 g fat: 60 g (saturated fat: 35 g)

Chocolate Truffles

These delectable truffles are the perfect little mouthful to round off dinner with a black coffee or brandy. If you use a high-quality diabetic chocolate, no one will believe they're sugar-free. Wearing latex or plastic gloves makes rolling the truffle mixture easier. You will probably get through several changes of gloves.

8 ounces dark diabetic chocolate,
　　broken into pieces
3½ tablespoons butter
¾ cup heavy cream
⅓ cup unsweetened pure
　　cocoa powder

Makes 35

Place the chocolate in a food processor and pulse until very finely chopped.

Add the butter and cream to a pan over low heat and warm gently just until the butter has melted. Remove the pan from the heat and stir in the chocolate. Continue to stir until smooth. If the mixture is too hot, it may separate. If this happens, add more cream.

Pour the mixture into a flat dish that will fit in the refrigerator. Let cool, then chill until firm.

Place the cocoa powder in a large bowl. Remove the truffle mixture from the refrigerator. Prepare a few truffles at a time by scraping up cherry-sized lumps of mixture, rolling them into smooth balls, and dropping them into the bowl of cocoa. Shake them around in the cocoa to coat evenly, then transfer to a plate. Continue until you have used up all of the truffle mixture.

Chill the truffles until ready to use.

Per serving
Carbs: 3 g protein: 0.9 g calories: 71 fiber: 0 g fat: 6.3 g (saturated fat: 3.9 g)

Pistachio Meringues

These are very different from traditional meringues, but absolutely wonderful in their own right. They are feather-light and literally melt in the mouth while being crunchy at the same time. Pistachios make them extra special, but you could use hazelnuts or almonds instead.

¾ cup shelled pistachios

2 egg whites

Pinch of cream of tartar

⅓ cup sweetener

Makes 8

Preheat the oven to 250°F. Line a cookie sheet with parchment paper.

Grind the pistachios to a powder in a food processor or chop as finely as possible by hand. Beat the egg whites with cream of tartar in a grease-free bowl until stiff. Beat in the sweetener. Gently fold in the ground pistachios, keeping the mixture light and airy.

Spoon little mounds of the mixture onto the cookie sheet. Bake for 30–40 minutes, or until crisp and golden.

Per serving
Carbs: 1 g protein: 3 g calories: 78 fiber: 0.8 g fat: 7 g (saturated fat: 1 g)

Rhubarb Fool

Low-carb sweeteners taste particularly authentic with acidic foods, so rhubarb is a perfect foil and is itself low-carb. Ginger, also a great partner to rhubarb, makes this quintessentially English dessert complete.

**14 ounces rhubarb, trimmed
and cut into ½-inch pieces**

3 tablespoons water

2 teaspoons finely grated fresh ginger

Pinch of salt

¼ cup sweetener

1¼ cups heavy cream

Serves 6

Place the rhubarb, water, ginger, and salt in a nonreactive pan (that is, not aluminum). Cover and bring to a boil. Reduce the heat to a low simmer and stew for about 15 minutes, or until the rhubarb has collapsed. Strain off some of the liquid through a nonaluminum strainer, then place the rhubarb in a ceramic or glass bowl and let cool.

When cool, add sweetener to taste. Whip the cream until it holds its shape, then fold it into the rhubarb. Let it streak through the cream in pink ripples, but don't blend it in completely. Spoon into four glasses and chill for at least 30 minutes before serving.

Per serving
Carbs: 2 g protein: 2 g calories: 380 fiber: 1.5 g fat: 40 g (saturated fat: 25 g)

Eton Mess

Here's a rather nuttier version of the English summertime classic, made with Pistachio Meringues (see p.156). A touch of rosewater enhances the sweetness. Use strawberries instead of raspberries if that's what's available.

1 quantity Pistachio Meringues
   (see p.156)

1 cup heavy cream

1 cup raspberries

1 teaspoon rose water

Serves 6

Whip the cream until it holds its shape, but do not overwhip it.

Place the meringues in a large bowl and break them up slightly. Add the raspberries and cream and fold through, being careful not to flatten the meringues. Gently fold the rose water through the mixture. Serve immediately.

Per serving
Carbs: 3.3 g protein: 6 g calories: 484 fiber: 2.5 g fat: 49 g (saturated fat: 26 g)

09:
FLAVOR ESSENTIALS

A few basics, with dressings and sauces specially designed to inject flavor, color, and texture into just about anything that fails to excite. With these essential recipes in your repertoire, you can create your own low-carb dishes.

Vegetable Stock

Homemade vegetable stock will make your soups and stews taste better than a powder or cube, and will always be guaranteed virtually carb-less, if you follow my guidelines below. Alas, life doesn't always allow us the luxury of time to make it (although it only takes about half an hour). If you can make a large batch, however, freeze it in 1-cup portions in resealable plastic freezer bags. Also, save the water left from steaming and blanching vegetables and freeze it the same way.

Vegetables (see list below)
Water (quantity to suit)
Sea salt
Peppercorns

GOOD in stock:
Scallions
Garlic
Celery and celery leaves
Parsley and parsley stems
Leeks and well washed leek greens
Broccoli and broccoli stems
Zucchini
Fennel and fennel tops
Turnips
Woody herbs, such as rosemary and thyme
Bay leaves

AVOID in stock:
Cabbage, spring greens, collard greens, kale
Cauliflower
Brussels sprouts
Potatoes and any other starchy vegetables

Fill half a large Dutch oven or stockpot with items from the "Good" list. Add enough water to cover the vegetables. Add sea salt to taste and a small handful of peppercorns. Bring to a boil and simmer for 20–30 minutes, then strain. Use immediately, or cool and keep chilled for up to 3 days. Alternatively, freeze as described above.

Per 1¼ cup serving
Carbs: 0.8 g protein: 2 g calories: 16 fiber: 0 g fat: 0.2 g (saturated fat: 0 g)

Paneer

This homemade curd cheese is a staple of the Indian diet. It's high in protein and has a wonderful creamy yet chewy texture. It is sold in some supermarkets and Asian grocery stores, but when you discover how easy it is to make yourself, you'll be a convert—all you have to do is separate milk into curds and whey. The homemade stuff is also infinitely lighter and creamier.

6 pints whole milk

scant ½ cup strained freshly squeezed
   lemon juice

Makes about 10½ ounces

Bring the milk to a boil in a large pan. As soon as it starts to rise up the insides of the pan, turn off the heat. Stir in the lemon juice. Cover the pan and let stand for 10 minutes.

Drain the curds into a colander lined with muslin or a clean dish towel. When cool enough to handle, squeeze out the excess moisture and let cool and drain further, then chill.

Paneer can be used once it has cooled, although it will have a very crumbly texture. It will become firm enough to slice within 1 hour in the refrigerator, and will harden further the longer it's chilled.

Per 3-ounce serving
Carbs: 2 g protein: 9 g calories: 76 fiber: 0 g fat: 3 g (saturated fat: 1.5 g)

Blender Hollandaise

It's just about the most sinful sauce around—all that butter—but if you're sticking to your low-carb diet, a little of this won't blow it for you. This foolproof version has a particular affinity with steamed asparagus, and it's an essential part of Eggs Florentine (see p.28).

3 organic egg yolks

2 tablespoons water

1 tablespoon fresh lemon juice

1¼ sticks lightly salted butter, diced

Serves 4

Place the egg yolks, water, and lemon juice in a blender.

Place the butter in a pan over very low heat. As soon as it has melted, remove from the heat but do not let it cool.

Switch on the blender, then gradually pour the hot melted butter through the hole in the lid to produce a thick and creamy emulsion.

If the sauce needs to be kept for a short time before use, it can be poured into a heatproof bowl, covered, and set over a pan of hot water (not actively simmering) to keep warm. It will solidify if stored in the refrigerator, but reheats successfully in a microwave.

Per serving

Carbs: 0.2 g protein: 2 g calories: 325 fiber: 0 g fat: 35 g (saturated fat: 20 g)

Pesto

There's plenty else to enjoy pesto with, other than traditional pasta. Look for the amazing range of carb-free and low-carb pasta, noodles, and rice available online and in specialty suppliers. Try it stirred through spaghetti squash (see p.80 for cooking instructions), as a dressing for boiled turnips, pumpkin, or cauliflower, or as an uplifting companion for crunchy vegetables, such as celery (see Celery with Pesto, p.111).

Large bunch of fresh basil, stems and
    leaves, torn
⅔ cup pine nuts
2 garlic cloves
½ cup freshly grated Parmesan cheese
Salt
⅓ cup olive oil

Serves 4

Place the basil, pine nuts, garlic, Parmesan, and a pinch of salt in a food processor. Process until finely chopped, then, with the motor running, gradually add the oil. Taste for seasoning and add more salt if necessary. Store in an airtight container in the refrigerator for up to 3 days, or freeze.

Per serving
Carbs: 1 g protein: 9 g calories: 382 fiber: 0.5 g fat: 38 g (saturated fat: 6 g)

Raspberry Purée

This pink purée poses as a sweet sauce, flavoring (see Zabaglione, p.150), or as a low-carb jam substitute (see Cottage Cheese Pancakes, p.31).

½ cup raspberries
1½ tablespoons water
1 tablespoon sweetener

Makes about ½ cup

Serves 4

Place all the ingredients in a blender and process until smooth. Pass through a strainer. The purée can be stored in the refrigerator for up to 3 days, or can be frozen.

Per serving
Carbs: 0.9 g protein: 0.3 g calories: 5 fiber: 0.5 g fat: 0.1 g (saturated fat: 0 g)

Sweet Chili Sauce

This basic sauce is a perfect balance of sweet, sour, salty, and hot—the principle behind that irresistible flavor of Southeast Asian food.

2 tablespoons fresh lime juice

2 tablespoons light soy sauce

2 tablespoons sweetener

2 small hot red chiles, minced

1 small garlic clove, crushed
   or finely grated

Serves 4

Combine all the ingredients. The heat will increase the longer it stands.

Per serving
Carbs: 0 g protein: 0.2 g calories: 3 fiber: 0.6 g fat: 0 g (saturated fat: 0 g)

Coconut Chili Sauce

This is a fantastic marinade for tofu or a quick way to liven up steamed vegetables. It's also delicious with hard-cooked eggs. It uses ready-made chili sauce so check the label to make sure it's a low-carb version with no sugar or modified starch.

5 tablespoons coconut milk or coconut
   cream

2 teaspoons low-carb chili sauce or
   several dashes of Tabasco sauce

2 teaspoons light soy sauce

1 teaspoon fresh lime juice

1 teaspoon sweetener

Serves 4

Mix all ingredients together and serve. The sauce may solidify if it is kept in the refrigerator; return to room temperature before use.

Per serving
Carbs: 1 g protein: 0.6 g calories: 35 fiber: 0 g fat: 3.2 g (saturated fat: 2 g)

Basic Vinaigrette

A heavy mortar and pestle is one of the most useful tools in the kitchen. Using a mortar and pestle, you will get the very best flavor out of garlic as the base for any vinaigrette or sauce.

1 garlic clove

1 teaspoon coarse sea salt

2 tablespoons white wine vinegar

1 teaspoon dry mustard

½ teaspoon mixed dried herbs
    or Herbes de Provence

Freshly ground black pepper

3 tablespoons extra virgin olive oil

Serves 4

Using a mortar and pestle, pound the garlic with the salt until a smooth paste forms. Using the pestle, work in the vinegar, mustard, and herbs, and season to taste with pepper. Gradually whisk in the olive oil.

Per serving

Carbs: 0 g protein: 0 g calories: 75 fiber: 0 g fat: 8 g (saturated fat: 1 g)

Cheese Sauce

This rich sauce will make just about anything more exciting—try it ladled over a plate of steamed broccoli and zucchini with hard-cooked eggs or smoked tofu.

½ cup Vegetable Stock (see p.162)

heaping ⅓ cup cream cheese

scant ½ cup grated Gruyère, extra
    sharp cheddar, or other tangy
    cheese

½ teaspoon dry mustard (optional)

½ teaspoon fresh or dried thyme
    leaves
    (optional)

Serves 4

Bring the stock to a boil in a skillet. Add the cream cheese, breaking it up with a wire whisk. Whisk until smooth and melted.

Add the grated cheese, mustard, and thyme, if using, and whisk until the cheese has melted and the sauce is thick. Remove from the heat and serve immediately.

Per serving

Carbs: 0.4 g protein: 5 g calories: 165 fiber: 0 g fat: 16 g (saturated fat: 10 g)

Italian Blue Cheese Dressing

The true, original blue cheese dressing—before it came out of labeled bottles—for all kinds of salads. Make sure the cheese is room temperature before you start.

3½ ounces Gorgonzola cremosa, Dolcelatte, or other soft blue cheese

1 tablespoon white wine vinegar

2 tablespoons extra-virgin olive oil

Sea salt and freshly ground black pepper

Makes about 3½ fluid ounces

Serves 4

Remove and discard any rind from the cheese. Place the cheese in a bowl and break it up slightly with a fork, then beat in the vinegar. Beat in the oil with a pinch of salt and pepper. This dressing will keep in the refrigerator for up to 3 days.

Per serving
Carbs: 0.2 g protein: 6 g calories: 152 fiber: 0 g fat: 14 g (saturated fat: 6.5 g)

Sesame Vinaigrette

A light salad dressing with an Asian twist, this is also a good tofu marinade.

1 tablespoon sesame seeds

2 tablespoons dark soy sauce

2 tablespoons rice vinegar

2 tablespoons sesame oil

Makes about 3½ fluid ounces

Serves 4

Place the sesame seeds in a small, dry skillet and set over medium heat. Cook, shaking the pan and stirring frequently, until the seeds are popping and golden. Transfer to a bowl and let cool.

Beat the remaining ingredients into the toasted sesame seeds. Use immediately, while the seeds are still crunchy.

Per serving
Carbs: 0.6 g protein: 1 g calories: 75 fiber: 0.3 g fat: 8 g (saturated fat: 1 g)

Sesame Mayo

Here's an example of how the magical combination of three ingredients adds up to more than the sum of its parts. This versatile sauce/dressing/dip just goes with everything!

3 tablespoons sesame seeds
½ cup mayonnaise
1½ tablespoons dark soy sauce

Makes ½ cup

Serves 4

Place the sesame seeds in a small, dry skillet and set over medium heat. Cook, shaking the pan and stirring frequently, until the seeds are popping and golden. Transfer to a bowl and let cool.

Add the mayonnaise and soy sauce and combine thoroughly. The sauce is best eaten on the day you make it, because the sesame seeds tend to get soggy after a while.

Carbs: 0.3 g protein: 1 g calories: 137 fiber: 0.3 g fat: 15 g (saturated fat: 2 g)

Satay Sauce

This sauce or dressing provides a speedy flavor injection. Make a quick *Gado-Gado* salad with hard-cooked eggs, lettuce, or shredded cabbage, beansprouts, a few bell pepper strips, and sliced scallion, then smother it in this dressing.

3 tablespoons crunchy natural peanut
    butter
2 tablespoons boiling water
2 teaspoons low-carb ready-made
    chili sauce
1 teaspoon fresh lime juice
1 teaspoon sweetener
Soy sauce, to taste (optional)

Makes about 3½ fluid ounces

Place the peanut butter in a small bowl and add the boiling water. Beat with a fork until thoroughly combined. Beat in the remaining ingredients and taste for seasoning. Beat in a little soy sauce for extra saltiness, if desired.

Per serving
Carbs: 1 g protein: 2 g calories: 50 fiber: 0.5 g fat: 4 g (saturated fat: 1 g)

MENU
IDEAS

BRUNCH BUFFET
Japanese Omelet, *p.25*
Blueberry Almond Griddle Cakes, *p.18*
Almond Muffins with Butter, *p.33*
Melon Berry Power Smoothie, *p.21*
Black Coffee

MEDITERRANEAN MEZE
Olive Raisins, *p.100*
Halloumi-stuffed Bell Peppers, *p.48*
Smoked Eggplant Purée, *p.125*
Chile Citrus Labneh Platter, *p.122*
Fruity Red Wine

AL FRESCO LUNCH
Spanish Tortilla with Zucchini and Manchego, *p.66*
Green Bean and Roasted Bell Pepper Parcels, *p.116*
A Crisp Green Salad Served with Italian Blue Cheese Dressing, *p.168*
Chilled Prosecco

PICNIC
Tunisian Spiced Torte, *p.84*
Marinated Crudité Salad, *p.110*
Cream Cheese and Macadamia Nut Brownies, *p.152*
Iced Tea with Lemon and Sweetener

LUNCH BUFFET
Portobello Mushrooms with Blue Cheese Custard, *p.46*
Provençal Tian, *p.89*
Avocado and Lemon Salad, *p.128*
Chocolate Marzipan Cheesecake, *p.144*

EASY ASIAN BUFFET
Tofu, Mint, and Palm Heart Salad, *p.60*
Vietnamese Asparagus Pancakes, *p.70*
Gado-Gado Salad, see Satay Sauce intro, *p.169*
Coconut Ice Cream, *p.146*

LUNCH BOX
Spanish Tortilla with Zucchini and Manchego, *p.66*
Spicy Tofu Biltong, *p.106*
Almond Muffin, *p.33*

WARMING WINTER LUNCH
Curried Celeriac Soup with Cilantro Oil, *p.56*
Warm Eggplant Salad with Melting Camembert, *p.75*
Zabaglione, *p.150*

SPEEDY AFTER-WORK DINNER 1
Chinese-Spice Tofu and Baby Leaf Salad, *p.59*
Egg Foo Yung, *p.86*

SPEEDY AFTER-WORK DINNER 2
Egg Flower Soup, *p.40*
Warm Exotic Mushroom Salad, *p.62*

THAI FEAST
Cucumber and Tofu Satay, *p.118*
Fragrant Coconut Broth, *p.36*
Thai Hot and Sour Salad with Crispy Tofu, *p.78*
Coconut Ice Cream, *p.146*
Jasmine Tea

INDIAN FEAST
Spiced Charred Eggplant, *p.51*
Paneer and Herb Fritters, *p.92*
Pumpkin and Egg Curry, *p.94*
Rose and Raspberry Pudding, *p.154*
Low-Carb Beer

COCKTAIL BASH
Chile-Crust Brazil Nuts, *p.100*
Saffron Aïoli with Quail Eggs and Asparagus, *p.120*
Eggplant and Smoked Cheese Involtini, *p.114*
Cucumber with Pink Pickled Ginger, *p.117*
Chocolate Truffles, *p.155*
Vodka Martinis

FOUR-COURSE RED-CARPET DINNER
Tricolore Skewers (with Champagne), *p.117*
Red Bell Pepper and Goat Cheese Timbales, *p.45*
Warm Poached Egg Salad with Tarragon Vinaigrette, *p.64*
Chilled White Burgundy
Individual Berry Gratins, *p.142*
Cognac and Black Coffee

INDEX

For Christiane Kubrick

METRO BOOKS
New York

An Imprint of Sterling Publishing
387 Park Avenue South
New York, NY 10016

© 2014 Anova Books Company Limited
Text © 2014 Celia Brooks
Illustrations © 2014 Anova Books Company Limited

This 2014 edition published by Metro Books by arrangement with Anova Books Company Limited.

Photographer: Clare Winfield (except pp.32, 44, 74, 88, 96 by Tara Fisher)

ISBN 978-1-4351-5171-0

For information about custom editions, special sales, and premium and corporate purchases, please contact Sterling Special Sales at 800-805-5489 or specialsales@sterlingpublishing.com.

Manufactured in China

2 4 6 8 10 9 7 5 3 1

www.sterlingpublishing.com